高职高专"十三五"规划教材

民航运输类专业系列教材

民航客舱服务英语综合教程

MINHANG KECANG FUWU YINGYU ZONGHE JIAOCHENG

王丽娟　杨　丹　主　编
孙　梅　副主编
Angus Cargill　主　审

化学工业出版社
·北京·

《民航客舱服务英语综合教程》以培养空乘人员英语综合能力为核心,以空中乘务工作四阶段为主线,分成15个工作场景,各个场景单元紧密衔接,基本涵盖了乘务员客舱服务流程,其中包括航前准备、航前检查、登机和问候、起飞前、酒水服务、餐食服务、娱乐服务、免税商品销售服务、机上急救、安全和紧急情况、航班特殊情况、乘客问询、降落前检查、降落之后以及航后讲评等主要环节。为方便教学和学生学习,每个单元都配有与教学内容相关的音频文件(以二维码形式,扫码即可打开),并配有电子课件。

本书可作为高职高专院校航空服务类专业学生的教材,也可作为航空公司在职人员提高素质的书籍,也可以作为航空培训参考用书或者自学用书。

图书在版编目(CIP)数据

民航客舱服务英语综合教程/王丽娟,杨丹主编.—北京:化学工业出版社,2018.8(2025.2重印)
高职高专"十三五"规划教材
ISBN 978-7-122-32605-8

Ⅰ.①民… Ⅱ.①王…②杨… Ⅲ.①民用航空-旅客运输-商业服务-英语-高等职业教育-教材 Ⅳ.①F560.9

中国版本图书馆CIP数据核字(2018)第152166号

责任编辑:旷英姿　　　　　　　　　　文字编辑:李　曦
责任校对:王　静　　　　　　　　　　装帧设计:王晓宇

出版发行:化学工业出版社(北京市东城区青年湖南街13号　邮政编码100011)
印　　装:北京科印技术咨询服务有限公司数码印刷分部
787mm×1092mm　1/16　印张11½　字数262千字　2025年2月北京第1版第6次印刷

购书咨询:010-64518888　　　　　　　售后服务:010-64518899
网　　址:http://www.cip.com.cn
凡购买本书,如有缺损质量问题,本社销售中心负责调换。

定　　价:32.00元　　　　　　　　　　　　　　　　版权所有　违者必究

前 言

航空业的日趋国际化对空中乘务人员的英语听、说、读、写、译能力提出了更高的要求，具备良好的乘务英语综合能力是每位空乘人员不可或缺的一种职业素质，它直接关系到航空公司的服务质量以及形象。然而，作为从事空乘英语教学多年的一线教师，我们在实践中发现很多教材功能单一，多侧重于会话操练或者听力训练，忽略了读者英语听、说、读、写和译综合能力提高，因而在教学实践中常常需要补充其他材料以弥补现有教材的不足。

本书是基于作者多年空中乘务英语教学实践，以培养空乘人员英语综合能力为核心，以空中乘务工作的四个阶段(预先准备、直接准备、飞行实施和航后讲评)为主线，分成15个工作场景，各个场景单元紧密衔接且内容翔实，基本涵盖了乘务员客舱服务流程，其中包括航前准备、航前检查、登机和问候、起飞前、酒水服务、餐食服务、娱乐服务、免税商品销售服务、机上急救、安全和紧急情况、航班特殊情况、乘客问询、降落前检查、降落之后以及航后讲评等主要环节。每个单元分成七部分，内容及功能介绍如下：

第一部分为听力训练：该部分旨在培养读者听的能力，由视频和听力两部分组成。读者可以通过观看真实场景下的视频节目，对该工作场景有直观和感性的认识，然后通过听力练习，提高自己的听力水平。

第二部分为情景对话：该部分旨在培养读者说的能力。该部分包含工作场景中比较实用的4~6个对话，对话后面有重点词汇和词组解释以及难点说明。本部分是各单元最重要的部分，建议读者熟练掌握，灵活运用。

第三部分为语言训练：该部分旨在强化听说部分出现的重点句型、句子结构和情景，听说练相结合。建议读者熟练掌握重点句型及常用表达。

第四部分为广播词练习：该部分旨在培养读者的中英文广播词朗读能力及语音语调。该部分依据国内外民用航空中的常用机上广播内容进行编写。建议读者能用标准的语音、语调及语速朗读广播词。

第五部分为面试英语：该部分旨在提高读者的航空面试能力。通过向读者提供面试时经常会碰到的问题及答案，帮助读者顺利通过航空面试，成为一名合格的客舱服务人员。

第六部分为补充词汇：该部分补充了书中没有出现但是在实践当中会出现的高频词汇，学有余力的读者可熟练掌握。

第七部分为阅读材料：该部分旨在培养读者的阅读和自学能力。读者可自学。

本书可作为高职高专院校航空服务类专业学生的教材，也可作为航空公司在职人员提高素质的书籍，也可以作为航空培训的参考用书。本书每一单元都配有与教学内容相关的音频二维码，音频由母语为英语的外教 Angus Cargill、Ann MurPhy 朗读，可供读者进行练习和模仿。本书亦可作为本科航空专业或者非航空专业学生自学用书。

本书由上海建桥学院王丽娟和杨丹担任主编，孙梅任副主编；上海建桥学院王重华、Conor 陈梁（外教），东华大学吴蕾参编；Angus Cargill 担任主审。在此感谢中国国际航空公司、中国东方航空股份有限公司、海南航空控股股份有限公司、上海吉祥航空股份有限公司、春秋航空股份有限公司、阿联酋航空公司等多位专家对本书编写的指导和帮助。

另外，若读者需要与本书相关的视频教学文件，可向编者发邮件索取，电子邮箱为 37500699@qq.com。

由于时间仓促，疏漏和不足之处在所难免，恳请有关专家和读者指正，并提出宝贵意见，我们一定会不断修订，不断完善。

编者

2018 年 4 月

Content（目录）

民航客舱服务英语综合教程

1 CHAPTER　Preliminary Flight Preparation　Page
（预先准备阶段）　1
Unit 1　Preflight Briefing（航前准备） ·· 2

2 CHAPTER　Preflight Preparation　Page
（直接准备阶段）　13
Unit 2　Preflight Check（航前检查） ·· 14

3 CHAPTER　Flight Procedures　Page
（飞行实施阶段）　23
Unit 3　Boarding and Greetings（登机和问候） ························ 24
Unit 4　Before Take-off（起飞前） ·· 33
Unit 5　Beverage Service（酒水服务） ······································ 42
Unit 6　Meal Service（餐食服务） ·· 52
Unit 7　Entertainment Service（娱乐服务） ······························ 62
Unit 8　Duty-free Service（免税商品销售服务） ······················ 70
Unit 9　First Aid（机上急救） ·· 79
Unit 10　Safety and Emergencies（安全和紧急情况） ·············· 88
Unit 11　Flight Irregularities（航班特殊情况） ·························· 97
Unit 12　Enquiries（乘客问询） ·· 105
Unit 13　Prelanding Check（降落前检查） ································ 113
Unit 14　After Landing（降落之后） ·· 120

4 CHAPTER　Flight Debriefing　Page
（航后讲评阶段）　129
Unit 15　Crew Debriefing（航后讲评） ······································ 130

Appendix
（附录） ... 137

Appendix 1　Glossary（附录 1　词汇表） 138
Appendix 2　Supplementary Vocabulary（附录 2　补充词汇表）............... 152
Appendix 3　Answer Key（附录 3　答案）............... 160
Appendix 4　Listening Transcript（附录 4　听力文本）............... 169

References
（参考文献） ... 177

Chapter 1

Preliminary Flight Preparation

（预先准备阶段）

Unit 1 Preflight Briefing
（航前准备）

Section One Listening

Phrases in Listening

preflight briefing 航前准备会
reduce the risk 减少风险
emergency procedures 紧急程序
organize workload 安排工作
individual question 一对一问题
communicate information 交流信息
cabin crew manual 乘务员手册
aviation first aid 机上急救
safety and emergency procedure 安全和紧急程序
potential nose gear collapse 潜在前起落架故障

Ⅰ. **Watch the video entitled Preflight Briefing and discuss the following questions in pairs:**

1. What are these people?
2. What kind of meeting are they having?
3. What are they talking about at the meeting?

Ⅱ. **Listen to the passage and fill in the missing words.**

What do cabin crew discuss at the preflight briefing?

1. A successful briefing creates an action plan for the day, communicating information between crew members and checking that we are all on the same page and reducing the _____ of incidents during the flight.

2. When you arrive at your base, you will check in and make sure there are no changes to your _____ and collect any safety updates or company news. It is also wise to check your cabin crew manuals for a quick reminder of safety and emergency procedures and aviation first aid.

3. The senior cabin crew member (SCCM) will check with you that have your required items: ID, passport, _____ and introduce themselves—their task is to organize

the workload and make sure the cabin crew know their responsibilities.

4. At the briefing, you will meet your SCCM and your fellow cabin crew for the flight. The SCCM will either _____ your position on the aircraft for the flight (e.g. Door 1 left or R4 for example) or the most senior crew member will choose a position and then the next most senior will choose until all crew members have a working position.

5. You will then go through a safety and _____ procedures (SEP) as a team and then be asked individual questions—for example, a potential nose gear collapse on landing and how you would prepare yourself, the cabin and the passengers for a preplanned emergency evacuation.

Section Two Conversations

Dialogue 1 Greetings and Self-introduction

Purser: Good morning, everyone. May I have your attention, please? Shall we begin our preflight briefing?

All: OK, we are ready.

Purser: Welcome to CA853 flight to Paris. For those who haven't flown with me, my name's Johnny Chen. I'm the chief purser in charge of today's flight. I have 10 year flying experience. I'd like to introduce your cabin supervisors. Anna Wang is going to be in charge of Business Class today and Amy Liu is in charge of Economy Class. Have you met before?

Anna: Yes. Hello, everyone.

Amy: Hi, everyone. It's nice to see some new and familiar faces.

Purser: And I see we have 3 longhaul crew members joining us today. I'd like to introduce them, this is Charles Huang and this is Peter Li. And she is Erica Fang.

Charles: Hi, nice to meet you.

Peter: Pleased to meet you.

Erica: How do you do!

Anna: Welcome to join us!

Purser: May I see your travel documents, please?

All: Sure. Here they are.

Amy: Charles and Peter, we'll work together. If you are not sure of any of your responsibilities, don't hesitate to ask us, we will be glad to help you out.

Peter: Thanks. I'm excited about my first long-haul flight.

Dialogue 2 Flight Time, Distance and Weather

Purser: Let's begin our briefing. We are flying an Airbus A320 today. Flight

CA853 is a direct flight, departing from Pudong International Airport at 0:15 a.m. and arriving at Charles de Gaulle International Airport at 6:40 a.m., local time. The flight time is 13 hours and 20 minutes. It will fly over China, Mongolia, Russia, Finland, Switzerland, Germany, Belgium and France.

Peter: Can I clarify something? What is the distance from Shanghai to Paris?

Purser: Well, it is about 9000 kilometers.

Charles: What about the cabin service today?

Purser: Cabin service in today's flight is drinks service with light meal and breakfast. Anna, can you tell me the weather conditions in Paris today?

Anna: Well, according to the latest weather report, Paris will see a high of 24 degrees centigrade or 76 degrees Fahrenheit and sunny.

Dialogue 3   Passenger Information

Purser: Now let's discuss the passenger information on board. Amy, can you tell me how many passengers are checked in Business Class and Economy Class?

Amy: We have 8 passengers checked in Business Class and 150 passengers in Economy Class.

Purser: Could you tell me something about the special passengers, Anna?

Anna: We have one VIP on 3A Business Class and two vegetarians in Economy Class. And we have a gentleman in a wheelchair and he's been allocated seat number 27C. He'll board first, ahead of other passengers.

Purser: Yes, don't forget he will need an individual safety briefing. Just let me know if you have any problems.

Amy: Sure.

Dialogue 4   Safety and Emergency Procedures

Purser: Let's go over the safety and emergency procedures. If our aircraft is entering an area of turbulence, what will you do, Charles?

Charles: I will remind the passengers to remain in their seats and fasten their seatbelts and the passengers who are in toilets should hold fast to the handles. Those passengers who are in the aisle should return to their seats and fasten their seatbelts. And cabin crew should secure the cabin equipment.

Purser: If you come across passengers who are using mobile power banks (charge pal) during the flight, what will you do, Amy?

Amy: I will go and persuade them to stop using charge pal and keep a close eye during the flight.

Purser: What will you do if the lithium battery is on fire?

Amy: I will attack the fire with the nearest water base extinguisher or using bottled water at hand immediately.

Purser: Great!

Words in the Conversation

briefing [ˈbriːfɪŋ] n. 准备会	purser [ˈpɜːsə (r)] n. 乘务长
attention [əˈtenʃn] n. 注意	responsibility [rɪˌspɒnsəˈbɪləti] n. 责任
hesitate [ˈhezɪteɪt] v. 犹豫	clarify [ˈklærəfaɪ] v. 使清楚
centigrade [ˈsentɪɡreɪd] a. 摄氏的	fahrenheit [ˈfærənhaɪt] a. 华氏温度计的
wheelchair [ˈwiːltʃeə (r)] n. 轮椅	allocate [ˈæləkeɪt] v. 分配；分派
individual [ˌɪndɪˈvɪdʒuəl] a. 个人的	procedure [prəˈsiːdʒə (r)] n. 程序
persuade [pəˈsweɪd] v. 说服	lithium [ˈlɪθiəm] n. 锂
extinguish [ɪkˈstɪŋɡwɪʃ] v. 熄灭	seatbelt [siːtbelt] n. 安全带
fasten [ˈfɑːsn] v. 系牢	

Useful Expressionas

chief purser 主任乘务长	in charge of 主管；负责
travel document 旅行证件	Charles de Gaulle International Airport 戴高乐国际机场
weather report 天气预报	charge pal 充电宝
keep a close eye 留心，注意	at hand 在手边；在附近
Business Class 商务舱	Economy Class 经济舱
long-haul flight 长途航班	

Notes

1. 乘务员有多种说法，可以为 cabin attendant 或者 flight attendant，无性别之分。
   steward 男空乘；stewardess 女空乘；air hostess 空中小姐（以前的称谓）。
   民航其他工作人员称呼如下：captain 机长 ; pilot 飞行员；copilot 副驾驶员；flight engineer 飞行机械师；navigator 领航员；purser/chief attendant 乘务长；chief purser 主任乘务长；ground crew 地勤人员；air crew 空勤人员；ground service staff 地面服务人员。

2. CA853，CA 为国航的两字代码，853 为航班号。读法如下：
   CA853 CA eight five three
   CA101 CA one zero one
   CA220 CA two two zero

3. 时间的说法：
   0:15   zero fifteen a.m.

8:20   eight twenty a.m.

16:35   four thirty five p.m.

18:55   six fifty five p.m.

4. Aircraft type 机型的读法：

     A330-200   Airbus three thirty dash two hundred

     A321   Airbus three twenty one

     B747   Boeing seven four seven

     B747-8   Boeing seven four seven dash eight

5. long-haul flight 长途航班

    medium-haul flight 中程航班

    short-haul flight 短途航班

6. 航班上的餐别

    breakfast 早餐

    lunch 午餐

    dinner 晚餐

    refreshment 点心

    light meal 轻正餐

    snack 小吃

Section Three   Language Practice

Ⅰ. **Substitution Drills**

Read the following sentences and do the same orally with the given phrases.

1. ***Anna Wang*** is going to be in charge of ***Business Class*** and ***Amy Liu*** is in charge of ***Economy Class***.

    a. Lucy—First Class—Peter—Economy Class

    b. Amy—first 4 rows—Ted—the middle 3 rows

    c. Jenifer—Exit 2—Tom—Exit 3

    d. Mary—the galley—Frank—the lavatory

2. ***Flight CA 853*** is a ***direct flight***, departing from ***Shanghai at 0:15*** a.m. and arriving at ***Charles de Gaulle International Airport at 6:40*** p.m.

    a. Flight CA1301—an evening flight—Beijing at 2:30 p.m.—Guangzhou at 5:35 p.m.

    b. Flight CA929—a daily flight—Shanghai on Tuesday—Frankfurt on Wednesday

    c. Flight MU721—a non-stop flight—Shanghai at 8:15a.m.—Hong Kong at 11:00p.m.

    d. Flight CZ600—an indirect flight—Shanghai at 1:45—New York at 23:00 by way of Guangzhou.

3. According to the latest weather report, ***Paris*** will see a high of ***24 degrees centigrade***

or 76 degrees Fahrenheit and sunny.

a. Moscow—minus 5 degrees centigrade or 23 degrees Fahrenheit—snowy

b. Los Angeles—10 degrees centigrade or 50 degrees Fahrenheit—cloudy

c. Sydney—5 degrees centigrade or 41 degrees Fahrenheit—sunny

d. Melbourne—minus 2 degrees centigrade or 28 degrees Fahrenheit—rainy

II. Quick responses

Look at the model and make quick and proper responses to the following inquiries.

Model: Purser: May I see your documents, please?
　　　　CA: Sure. Here they are.

1. Purser: Let's begin our briefing. I am the purser of this flight.
   CA: _____

   Purser: Have you met each other before?
   CA: _____

2. Purser: I'd like you to meet Mr. Brown.
   CA: _____

3. Purser: Could you tell me the weather conditions in Hong Kong today?
   CA: _____

4. Purser: Could you tell me something about the special passengers on this flight?
   CA: _____

5. Purser: Who is responsible for Exit 2?
   CA: _____

III. Role Play

1. Today is the first day of your career as a cabin attendant. You are at the preflight briefing of CA158 from Shanghai to Tokyo. Your chief purser Jennifer is going to give some flight information and assign the tasks. Work in groups.

2. You are a flight attendant with an English-speaking crew flying to Chicago. You have listened to all the details but you're still not sure about the departure time, gate number and flying time. Work in groups.

IV. Translate the following sentences into English

1. 我们可以开始航前准备会了吗？

   _____

2. 欢迎乘坐飞往巴黎的 CA853 航班。

   _____

3. 我是今天的主任乘务长。我有 10 年的飞行经验了。
   _____

4. 如果你们不确定自己的职责,尽管来问我,我很乐意帮助你们。
   _____

5. CA853 航班是直飞航班,凌晨 0:15 从浦东机场起飞,当地时间 6:40 降落在戴高乐国际机场。
   _____

6. 今天飞机上的客舱服务主要是早餐、午餐和饮料服务。
   _____

7. 根据最新的天气预报,巴黎是晴天,最高温度 24 摄氏度或者说 74 华氏度。
   _____

8. 我们有商务舱乘客 12 位,经济舱乘客 260 位。
   _____

9. 如果飞机进入颠簸区域,我会提醒乘客坐在座椅上并系好安全带。
   _____

10. 如果锂电池着火你怎么办?
    _____

Section Four Announcements

Welcome

Good morning/afternoon/evening, Ladies and Gentlemen,

This is your flight attendant Andy Han. On behalf of China Eastern Airlines, I'd like to welcome you aboard our Boeing 777 flight MU577 from Shang hai to Los Angeles.

Our captain today is Alan Smith, and cabin crew in charge is Jessica Li. The flight time is 12 hours and 5 minutes.

Thank you for choosing China Eastern Airlines and we wish you a pleasant flight!

Section Five Interview English

Personal Information

Ⅰ. **About your name**
   关于姓名

Q1: May I have your name, please? /What is your name, please? /Would you mind telling me your name?

你叫什么名字?

A: My name is Wang Yan.

You can call me Wang Yan.

My full name is Wang Yan.

Q2: What is your family name/surname?

你姓什么?

A: My family name/surname is Wang.

Q3: Do you have an English name?

你有英文名吗?

A: Yes, sir/madam. It is Amy. It was given by my English teacher when I was at college.

Sorry, I don't have an English name.

Ⅱ. **About your age**

关于年龄

Q1: When were you born? /May I know your birth date?

你什么时候出生的?

A: I was born on May 12, 1998.

My birth date is May 12, 1998.

Ⅲ. **About your hometown**

关于家乡

Q1: Where is your hometown?

你家乡是哪里?

A: My hometown is Shanghai.

I am from Shanghai.

Q2: Where is your birthplace?

你出生在哪里?

A: My birthplace is Shanghai.

My native place is Shanghai.

Q3: What is your nationality?

你的国籍是哪里?

A: I am Chinese.

I am an American by birth.

Section Six Supplementary Vocabulary

captain ['kæptɪn] n. 机长   preliminary [prɪ'lɪmɪnəri] a. 预备的

> nationality [ˌnæʃəˈnæləti] n. 国籍
> celsius [ˈselsiəs] n. 摄氏
> cabin attendant 乘务员
> flight route 飞行线路
> arrival time 到达时间
> departure time 出发时间；离港时间
> First Class 头等舱
> aircraft type 机型

Section Seven Self Study Reading

Objectives of Crew Briefings

Briefing should provide a clear picture of the flight ahead and build a common understanding of the expectations of the flight amongst the crew. A successful briefing should be short, interesting and detailed, and should include teamwork, communication, coordination, planning and anticipating possible unplanned events:

- Team Building and Teamwork

Many cabin crew and flight crew are faced with the challenge of constantly working with different colleagues, often with colleagues that they have never met or worked with before. However, they are expected to work in very close proximity for long periods of time. For a team to be successful, they must be able to talk to each other, share information, listen to each other and be assertive, when necessary.

- Encourage Open Communication

A good briefing must encourage open, interactive communication between all crewmembers, emphasize the importance of questions, input from crewmembers and Changing information.

- Crew Coordination and Workload Distribution

The briefing establishes the chain of command, the leadership. The purser organizes the workload and duties of the cabin crew and ensures that the cabin crewmembers understand their responsibilities. The workload must be evenly distributed amongst the crewmembers to avoid individuals suffering from work overload, which may distract attention from critical tasks and lead to errors.

- Planning and Time Management

Cabin crew activities should be planned, based on the flight time, the expected flight conditions, the Standard Operating Procedures of the Operator and the service requirements. Cabin crewmembers should be encouraged to prioritize tasks during periods of heavy workload, and according to flight conditions.

- Unplanned Events

Briefings are the ideal moment for cabin crew and flight crew to discuss the importance of safety duties and responsibilities, to ensure crew communication, coordination and crew awareness during unplanned events.

Chapter 2

Preflight Preparation

（直接准备阶段）

Unit 2 Preflight Check
（航前检查）

Section One   Listening

Phrases in Listening

flight crew 机务组
compulsory meeting 必开会议
board the aircraft 登机
stow away their baggage 存放行李
crew station 乘务员号位
emergency equipment checklist 紧急设备检查清单
security check 安全检查

cabin crew 乘务组
aviation authority regulation 民航局规定
assigned stations 指定号位
emergency equipment check 紧急设备检查
write all discrepancie 写下所有偏差状况
catering item 餐饮物品
suspicious item 可疑物品

Ⅰ. Watch the video entitled Preflight Check and discuss the following questions in pairs：
What equipment should the cabin crew check？

Ⅱ. Listen to the information about preflight check and decide which of these things you do just before the passengers come on board？ Put a "√" in the box.

☐1. Go to the assigned stations.

☐2. Help the passengers put their baggage in the overhead lockers.

☐3. Check the emergency equipment at their crew station, in lavatories, in overhead bins, in cupboards and under seats.

☐4. Change seats for passengers.

☐5. Check the uniform is smart.

☐6. Write any discrepancies on the emergency equipment checklist.

☐7. Make sure food and duty-free items are on board.

☐8. Count passenger meals and crew meals.

☐9. Check waste bins, galley lockers, trolleys and toilets.

☐10. Report any suspicious items to the senior crew member.

Section Two Conversations

CA1: Cabin Attendant 1   CA2: Cabin Attendant 2

Dialogue 1   Checking Crew Station

Purser: Hi, Lucy. Come here.

CA: Yes? What can I do for you, Purser?

Purser: I have seen the equipment listed on the Cabin Log Book (CLB). Would you please go and check Seat 21D to see if it is serviceable?

CA: Sure. Oh, it works!

Purser: OK. Now you should check the equipment which is at or around your crew station according to the checklist, and make sure all equipment is securely in position. Also check on the interphone and make sure it is functioning properly.

CA: All right.

Dialogue 2   Checking Demonstrator Life Jackets and Oxygen Masks

Purser: Excuse me, Lisa, are you busy now?

CA: Yes, I'm checking the demonstrator life jackets and oxygen masks. Is there anything else I can do for you?

Purser: I wonder if you can help me check the galley to see if all the equipment is ready to use.

CA: Sure.

Dialogue 3   Checking the Lavatory

CA1: Excuse me, are you going to check the front lavatory?

CA2: Yes.

CA1: You are supposed to check if there is anybody still inside the lavatory, amenities are in position and serviceable, the waste bin is clean, and the smoke detector and the flush buttons are working.

CA2: Okay, I will. Thank you.

Dialogue 4   Checking the Galley and Documents

CA1: Have you finished checking the galley?

CA2: No, not yet. I've just finished checking emergency equipment, oven and water heater. Next, I'm going to check the total portions and variety of drinks and food. How about you?

CA1: I've checked all the documents necessary for the flight are on the aircraft and arranged the magazines and newspaper in good order. Should I place magazines and timetables in the seat pockets?

CA2: I'm afraid not. You are supposed to put them in the magazine racks.

CA1: OK. I see.

Dialogue 5　Checking the Entertainment System

Purser：Hi, there, what are you doing now?

CA1：I've just checked all in-flight documents.

Purser：Please help me check the entertainment system, supplementary reading light, call button, video and audio, and speakers to see if they are functional.

CA1：OK.

Dialogue 6　Cabin Cleared

CA1：Purser, we've cleared the cabin. We've checked the safety and emergency equipment, the galley, the lavatory, wardrobes, baggage compartments, seats, seat back, seat pockets and so on.

Purser：All right. It's time to switch on the boarding music and welcome passengers to board the aircraft.

CA：Yes, Purser.

Words in the Conversation

equipment [ɪˈkwɪpmənt] n. 设备
checklist [ˈtʃeklɪst] n. 检查表
interphone [ˈɪntəfəʊn] n. 对讲机
galley [ˈɡæli] n. 机上厨房
amenity [əˈmiːnəti] n. 设施
portion [ˈpɔːʃn] n. 一部分
necessary [ˈnesəsəri] a. 必要的
supplementary [ˌsʌplɪˈmentri] a. 增补的
audio [ˈɔːdiəʊ] n. 音频
switch [swɪtʃ] vt. /n. 开关

serviceable [ˈsɜːvɪsəbl] a. 有用的
secure [sɪˈkjʊə(r)] a. 安全的；牢固的
functional [ˈfʌŋkʃənl] a. 起作用的
lavatory [ˈlævətri] n. 厕所
oven [ˈʌvn] n. 烤箱
document [ˈdɒkjumənt] n. 文件
arrange [əˈreɪndʒ] v. 整理
video [ˈvɪdiəʊ] n. 视频
wardrobe [ˈwɔːdrəʊb] n. 衣橱；衣柜
demonstrate [ˈdemənstreɪt] v. 演示；展示

Useful Expressions

Cabin Log Book (CLB) 客舱记录本
oxygen mask 氧气面罩
smoke detector 烟雾探测器
water heater 热水器
reading light 阅读灯
emergency equipment 紧急设备
magazine rack 杂志架
seat back 座椅靠背

demonstrator life jacket 示范用救生衣
waste bin 垃圾桶
flush button 冲水按钮
entertainment system 娱乐系统
call button 呼叫按钮
boarding music 登机音乐
seat pocket 座椅口袋

Notes

lavatory 洗手间，乘客也会说 toilet，restroom or W. C.。

Section Three Language Practice

Ⅰ. **Substitution Drills**

Read the following sentences and do the same orally with given phrases.

1. I wonder if you can help me check *the galley*.
   a. the total portions and quality of food
   b. the demonstrator life jackets and oxygen masks
   c. the in-flight magazines and newspapers
   d. the waste bin，the smoke detector and the flush button

2. Should I place *magazines and timetables in the seat pockets*?
   a. flight magazines in the seat pockets
   b. 3 bottles of mineral water in the galley
   c. the handcart in the rear cabin
   d. the bag in the lavatory

3. You are supposed to put them in the *magazine racks*.
   a. seat pockets
   b. front cabin
   c. fridge
   d. overhead compartment

Ⅱ. **Blank Filling**

Fill in the blanks with the words given below.

> stowed; up; variety; order; equipment

CA1：Hi，Miss Wang，what are you going to do?

CA2：I'm going to check the cabin to see if all the items in the seat pocket are in correct 1. _____, the seatbelts are crossed，tray tables are 2. _____，armrests are down，and all the window shades are 3. _____ and all the overhead compartments remain open. What are you busy with?

CA1：I've just finished checking emergency 4. _____. Next，I'm going to check the total portions and 5. _____ of drinks and food.

CA2：See you then.

CA1：See you.

Ⅲ. **Role Play**

1. Susan is checking the lavatory，and the purser comes to tell her what she should pay

attention to.

2. Lisa is checking the galley and Shirley is checking the documents. They are talking about their assigned work.

Ⅳ. Translate the following sentences into English.

1. 乘务长，我能为你做些什么吗？
   _____

2. 我正在检查示范用救生衣和氧气面罩。
   _____

3. 我想你是不是可以帮我查看一下厨房里面的设备是否已经准备好。
   _____

4. 你需要确认厕所里是否还有人。
   _____

5. 我刚刚检查完应急设备、烤箱和热水器。
   _____

6. 我已经把杂志和报纸摆放整齐了。
   _____

7. 我已经检查过所有机上需要的文件资料。
   _____

8. 请帮我查看一下娱乐系统，确保包括阅读灯、呼叫按钮、音频、视频和扬声器在内的设施都是可用的。
   _____

9. 现在可以打开登机广播，欢迎乘客登机了。
   _____

10. 乘务长，我们已经清理完客舱。
    _____

Section Four Announcements

Boarding

Ladies and Gentlemen,

Welcome aboard Air China. Please ask the cabin attendants if you cannot find your seat. The seat numbers are shown on the overhead locker/compartment/bins.

Please put your carry on baggage in the overhead locker or under the seat in front of you. Please keep the aisle and exits clear of all baggage.

Please take your assigned seats as quickly as possible and keep the aisle clear for others to be seated.

Thank you for your cooperation!

Boarding

Good morning/afternoon/evening, Ladies and Gentlemen,

We are honored to welcome you aboard Air China, a proud Star Alliance member.

Kindly store all your carry on luggage securely in the overhead bins or under the seat in front of you.

Please take your assigned seats as quickly as possible and leave the aisle clear for others to be seated.

We appreciate your cooperation. Thank you!

Section Five Interview English

Personal Information

Ⅰ. **About other related things**

其他信息

Q1: How about/is your health?

你的健康状况如何？

A: I'm in excellent health.

My health is very good.

I have always been in good health.

Q2: What is your blood type?

你的血型是什么？

A: It is type A/B/AB/O.

Q3: What is the motto/philosophy of your life?

你的座右铭/人生哲学是什么？

A: Nothing is impossible to a willing heart.

Good things always happen to those who smile.

Don't think about making the sea, you must start from small rivers.

Be brave, be kind, be honest and be faithful.

Ⅱ. **Self-Introduction**

Q: Would you please make a brief introduction to yourself?

你能简单介绍一下自己吗？

Good morning/afternoon, my name is xxx. It's my honor to take part in this interview. And I hope my performance today will please you. Now I will introduce myself briefly. I'm 21 years old and I will complete my three year college studies in June this year. My major is Civil Aviation Service. I have led 50 other students as the class monitor and implemented a lot of campus Youth Volunteers' activities. Among all the occupations I have considered, I am most attracted by becoming an airplane stewardess. Their charming temperament and elegant appearance make me even more eager to be one of them. I believe that my confidence can reassure all the passengers and my smile will make them feel the warmth of home. This is me. Thank you very much.

Section Six   Supplementary Vocabulary

cockpit ['kɒkpɪt] n. 驾驶员座舱
loudspeaker [ˌlaʊd'spiːkə(r)] n. 扬声器
life vest 救生衣
window shade 遮阳板
overhead compartment 座位上方的行李箱
life raft 救生筏
rear cabin 客舱后部

fridge [frɪdʒ] n. 电冰箱
handcart ['hændkɑːt] n. 手推车
tray table 小桌板
short haul flight 短途航班
assigned work 指定的工作

Section Seven   Self Study Reading

Pre flight Check

When an aircraft is cruising at 35000 feet, crew members cannot fix anything or replace equipment in an emergency. To avoid problems, we must always perform a preflight inspection on all emergency equipment. Here is a list of the most common emergency equipment that must be checked by the flight attendant, along with the procedure for checking each item:

- **Halon Fire Extinguishers**—Only classes A, B, or C. For preflight checking your halons, make sure they are securely fastened to the brackets and that the gauges are in the green. The pins should be secured and not tampered with.
- **Water Extinguisher**—Class A. For preflight checking your water extinguisher, make sure it is securely fastened to the brackets, that it has a CO_2 cartridge installed, and that the copper wire has not been tampered with.
- **Portable Oxygen Bottles (POB)**—For preflight checking your POBs, make sure they are full (between 1800~2000 PSI). If you have masks attached to them, make sure the hoses are in good working condition and the masks fit your face for quick donning.

The tubing should be connected to the high-flow valves, and the shoulder straps should be attached.
- **First Aid Kits**—Make sure your aircraft has a first aid kit on board and it is sealed for your flight. If it has been opened, make sure to restock it before your next flight.
- **Medical Kits**—Make sure your aircraft has a medical kit on board and it is sealed for your flight. These kits should only be opened in an emergency situation, and expired units should be updated and resealed yearly.
- **Defibrillator**—Check the defibrillator for damage or foreign substances. If it appears that the unit has been tampered with, immediately notify the Pilot in Command (PIC).
- **Protective Breathing Equipment (PBE) or Smoke Hood**—Make sure PBE is present and secure.

   Flashlights—Make sure you have a flashlight on board for your use. If it is attached to the aircraft, verify the red flashing light. If the flashlight is not attached to the aircraft, make sure the batteries are changed monthly. A good way to do this is to apply a sticker indicating the date when the batteries were replaced.
- **Life Vest**—Make sure there is a life vest for every seat and every crew member. The pouch should be sealed and not expired.
- **Life Raft**—Your life raft should be stowed, secured and inspected on every pre flight check. Check your raft for the dates when it has to be refurbished or inspected.
- **Seatbelts and Harnesses**—Double-check that all seatbelts are working properly and that shoulder harnesses are present and not hidden.
- **Megaphone**—Not all aircraft have to carry a megaphone, but if you have one, test it to make sure it's working. This piece of equipment is helpful in an emergency to gather everyone together and give important safety instructions.
- **Slide**—If you are flying on a large-cabin aircraft, you will have a slide for some of your exits. Make sure it is secure and can be armed properly. Check the type your aircraft is equipped with and locate the instructions on how to arm and unarm the door.
- **Emergency Lighting**—It is essential to double-check your emergency lighting to ensure it is clearly visible and all the lights are working.
- **Safety Information Cards**—Make sure you have the safety information cards readily available for your passengers to review in case of an emergency, as well as for your own review.

   As you can see, some emergency equipment is complex, and some is as simple as a flashlight, yet all of these items play a critical role in the event that an emergency arises.

Chapter 3

Flight Procedures

（飞行实施阶段）

Unit 3 Boarding and Greetings
（登机和问候）

Section One   Listening

Phrases in Listening

Business Class passengers 商务舱乘客	Bonjour, Monsiewr 您好，先生（法语）
our first priority 我们首要职责	block the way/aisle 挡住过道
in case of turbulence 万一发生颠簸	put the handcart 放手推车
in the front cabin 在前舱	in the cockpit 在驾驶舱
hurt somebody 伤到某人	the overhead bin/compartment 座位上方的行李箱

Ⅰ. **Watch the video entitled Boarding and Greetings and discuss the following questions in pairs：**

1. What did the cabin attendant say to welcome the passengers?
2. Which class did the passenger take，business or economy?
3. What drink did the cabir attendants offer before take-off?

Ⅱ. **Listen to the dialogue and choose the right answers.**

1. Why did the passenger put the handcart in the aisle? （   ）

    A． Because it was too big.

    B． Because the overhead compartment was full.

    C． Because he forgot to put it in the overhead compartment.

    D． Because it was too heavy.

2. Where did the flight attendant recommend to put the handcart? （   ）

    A． In the front cabin.

    B． In the cockpit.

    C． In the Business Class.

    D． Under the seat.

3. Why is it not recommended to put the handcart in the overhead compartment? (　　)

   A. Because it might fall off the compartment and hurt somebody.

   B. Because it will damage the overhead compartment.

   C. Because it should be put under the seat.

   D. Because it is too heavy.

Section Two　Conversations

PAX: Passenger　P1: Passenger 1　P2: Passenger 2　CA: Cabin Attendant

Dialogue 1　Welcome Aboard

CA: Good morning. Welcome aboard Air China!

PAX: Good morning. Where can I find my seat?

CA: May I see your boarding pass, please?

PAX: Here you are.

CA: Your seat number is 6C. Please go this way to the sixth row. The seat number is shown on the overhead compartment.

PAX: Thank you very much.

CA: You're welcome. Have a great flight!

Dialogue 2　Passengers with Baby Carriage

CA: Welcome on board! May I carry that bag for you?

PAX: Yes, please. I need your help.

CA: You may leave the baby carriage with me. I will give it back to you after we land at the destination airport.

PAX: Thank you. By the way, may I take another seat? I don't want to sit here. There isn't enough legroom to stretch out my legs.

CA: Would you please sit here for the time being? I'll see if there is a better seat.

PA: Thanks a lot.

CA: I'm sorry, but the economy class is fully booked. I'm afraid you will have to sit here.

PAX: All right.

Dialogue 3　Over-sized baggage

PAX: Miss, I don't know where to put my bag. The overhead compartment is full and I tried to put it under the seat, but it doesn't fit. Can you help me?

CA: Oh, your baggage is too big to be put in the overhead locker, I will ask the ground staff to check it for you. Please wait a moment.

CA: This is your checked baggage label. You may pick it up at the baggage claim area when we arrive.

PAX: OK, thanks.

CA: You are welcome!

Dialogue 4   Passenger in the Wrong Seat

P1: Excuse me, Miss. Someone is sitting in my seat.

CA: Could you please show me your boarding pass, please?

    Thank you. Just a moment, please.

    (To the passenger who is seated)

CA: Excuse me, Sir. May I see your seat number, please?

P2: Here you are.

CA: Thank you. I'm afraid you are sitting in the wrong seat. 16A is just in front of this one.

P2: Oh, I thought this was mine.

CA: Thank you for your cooperation. May I help you with your baggage?

P2: No thanks, I can manage myself.

CA: (To the waiting gentleman)

    Sorry for keeping you waiting, sir. Here is your seat.

P1: Thanks.

CA: No problem. Have a great trip!

Dialogue 5   Exchange Seat

P1: Miss, the man in 24D is my friend. Can I sit with him?

CA: Just a moment. I will talk with that gentleman in 24E.

CA: Excuse me, Sir. That gentleman over there is a friend of this young man beside you. They'd like to sit together. Would you mind changing seats with her?

P2: All right.

Dialogue 6   Baggage in the Aisle

CA: Excuse me, sir. Is this your bag?

PAX: Yes. Why?

CA: Would you mind keeping it under the seat, sir? I'm afraid we're not allowed to leave baggage here. It might block the aisle. Shall I put it under the seat, sir?

PAX: OK. That's fine.

CA: Many thanks for your cooperation. Have a nice trip!

Words in the Conversation

aboard [əˈbɔːd] v. 上（车、船、飞机）   destination [ˌdestɪˈneɪʃn] n. 目的地

legroom [ˈlegruːm] n. 伸腿的空间   stretch [stretʃ] v. 伸展；延伸

fit [fɪt] v. 适合   block [blɒk] v. 阻塞

Useful Expressions

welcome aboard 欢迎登机
boarding pass 登机牌
baby carriage 婴儿车
Economy Class 经济舱
fully booked 订满；客满
baggage label 行李标签

destination airport 目的地机场
seat number 座位号
for the time being 暂时
pick up 拿；取
ground staff 地勤人员 （亦可用 ground crew）
baggage claim area 行李认领处

Notes

1. boarding pass 登机卡，也可以称作 boarding card
2. in the front （of the cabin）在（客舱的）前部
   in the middle （of the cabin）在（客舱的）中部
   in the back （of the cabin）在（客舱的）后部
3. cockpit 驾驶舱（美）
   flight deck（英）
4. a window seat 靠窗座位
   aisle seat 靠过道座位
   middle seat 中间座位
5. overhead compartment 或者 overhead bin 座位上方的行李箱
   overhead rack 座位上方行李架
6. 向乘客指示方位：
   on the right/on the left 在右边/在左边
   on the right hand side/on the left hand side 在右手边/在左手边
   on one's right/on one's left 在某人右边/在某人左边
7. The Economy Class is fully booked. 经济舱满座了。也可以说：The Economy Class is full. There is no seat available in Economy Class.
8. baggage 行李，不可数名词。一件行李 a piece of baggage；两件行李 two pieces of baggage。行李也可以用 luggage。

Section Three Language Practice

I. Substitution Drills

Read the following sentences and do the same orally with the given phrases.

1. Good *morning*! Welcome aboard *Air China*!
   a. morning—China Eastern Airlines
   b. afternoon—Spring Airlines
   c. evening—Juneyao Airlines

d. afternoon—Air France

2. May I *see your boarding pass*, please?

   a. have your name and telephone number

   b. see your baggage tag

   c. have your name card

   d. see your ID card

3. Your seat number is 6C. Please *go this way to the sixth row*.

   a. go this way.

   b. wait a minute, and I will find it for you.

   c. go straight ahead. It is on your left.

   d. come with me. Here is 6 C.

4. Please *turn right*. Your seat is *in the middle of* the cabin, *a middle* seat.

   a. turn left—in the front of—an aisle seat

   b. turn right —in the rear of—a window seat

   c. go straight ahead—in the back of—a window seat

   d. go to the fifth row—in the middle of —a middle seat

5. I'm afraid you can't put your luggage *in the aisle*. You have to put it *under the seat*.

   a. in the first row—in the overhead compartment

   b. near the emergency exit—under your seat

   c. in the galley—in the overhead bin

   d. in the lavatory—in the front of the cabin

II. Quick responses

Look at the model and make quick and proper responses to the following inquiries.

Model: Purser: May I see your documents, please?

　　　　CA: Sure. Here they are.

1. PAX: Excuse me, Miss. Where can I find my seat?
   CA: _____

2. PAX: May I take another seat?
   CA: _____

3. CA: Could you please show me your boarding pass?
   PAX: _____

4. PAX: Can I sit with my friend?
   CA: _____

5. PAX: Excuse me, sir. I don't know where to put my bag.
   CA: _____

Ⅲ. **Role Play**

1. A passenger's seat number is 11C on a Boing 737-400. He doesn't know where his seat is. Please tell him how to find his seat.

2. A passenger has a baby carriage with her and it is blocking the cabin. What do you do in this situation?

3. A passenger is sitting in the wrong seat. What do you say to the passenger?

4. A passenger wants to sit with his friend. What do you say to the passenger?

Ⅳ. **Translate the following sentences into English**

1. 我能看一下您的登机牌吗？

2. 请沿着这条过道走到第6排。

3. 座椅号码标注在座位上方的行李箱上。

4. 没有足够的空间让我伸展我的腿。

5. 您的包太大，不能放在座位上方的行李箱内。

6. 经济舱预订满了。

7. 当我们到达后您可以去行李提取处领取托运行李。

8. 我恐怕您坐错位置了。

9. 您介意和她换个位置吗？

10. 您放在过道的行李会堵住路的。

Section Four Announcements

Boarding Pass Recheck

Ladies and Gentlemen,
 This is Air China flight CA1886 bound for Beijing. Would you please check your boarding pass once again and make sure of your flight number.
 Thank you for your cooperation!

Greetings

Good morning/afternoon/evening, Ladies and Gentlemen,
 Welcome aboard China Southern Airlines.
 I am Michael, the purser for this flight. During the flight, all of my colleagues will be happy to serve you. Thank you.
 We will take off in a few minutes. Please sit down and fasten your seatbelts. Please return your seat back and table to the upright position.
 All flights are non-smoking according to the government regulations. Please refrain from smoking during the flight.
 Thank you for your cooperation, and we wish you a pleasant journey!

Section Five Interview English

Ⅰ. **About Family**
 家庭情况

Q1: How many people/persons are there in your family? /How big is your family?
 你家有几口人?

A: There are three of us: my father, my mother and me. /There are four of us: father, mother, elder brother (sister) and me.

Q2: What does your father do? /What is your mother's occupation/job?
 你爸爸是做什么工作的? /你妈妈的职业是什么?

A: My father works in a bank. /He is an engineer.
 She is a doctor. /She is a housewife.

Q3: Please tell me something about your family.
 请说一说你家里情况。

A: My father does import and export business. My mother is a high school teacher. I am the only child in my family

There are four people in my family. My father works for the government. My mother is a housewife. I have a younger brother who is now studying in primary school.

Ⅱ. **About Education**

教育情况

Q1: Which college are you in? /Which college did you graduate from? /Which college will you graduate from?

你就读于哪所大学？/你毕业于哪所大学？/你将从哪所大学毕业？

A: I have been studying in _____ University for two years. /I graduated from _____ University. /I will graduate from _____ University.

Q2: What is/was your major?

你的专业是什么？

A: My major is/was Aviation Service/Flight Attendant/Cabin Attendant/Computer Science/Business Management.

I majored in Chemistry/Physics.

I am majoring in Nursing.

Q3: Why did you choose to learn Aviation Service?

你为什么选择学习航空服务专业？

A: Because I am interested in this field. I have liked the feeling of flying in the sky since I was very young and I am trying my best to make my dream come true.

Section Six   Supplementary Vocabulary

greetings [ɡˈriːtɪŋz] n. 问候
infant [ˈɪnfənt] n. 婴儿
terminal [ˈtɜːmɪnl] n. 候机楼
vacant [ˈveɪkənt] n. 空缺的
hand baggage 手提行李
cabin door 舱门
aisle seat 过道座位
charter flight 包机

assist [əˈsɪst] v. 协助；帮助
experienced [ɪkˈspɪəriənst] adj. 有经验的
airline [ˈeəlaɪn] n. 航空公司；航线

assigned seat 指定座位
flight crew 机组成员
window seat 靠窗座位
boarding procedure 登机手续

Section Seven   Self Study Reading

Passenger Boarding

At the time of the boarding, passengers, most of the time, are welcomed at the door of the airplane by the smiling faces of the cabin crew. The posture and their language must be positive to make the passengers impressed even before take-off. These will never know that behind the big smile, in fact, are hiding sometimes long hours of work. Cabin attendants have to perform the following tasks when passengers are boarding the aircraft:

- Inspect and monitor passenger boarding routes (including integral steps, external steps, piers and jetties) both prior to and during boarding to ensure that these remain safe.
- Monitor boarding to ensure no inadmissible passengers are permitted to board, including those who may be under the influence of alcohol and drugs.
- Observe passenger behavior and be aware of any suspicious behavior or items and report any security concerns immediately.
- Ensure passengers are advised of aircraft refueling and that both cabin crew and passengers comply with operator and regulatory procedures to ensure exits are manned and exit routes remain clear.
- Assist with passenger boarding and seating to ensure seating allocation is appropriate. Ensure that seats adjacent to exits are occupied by able-bodied passengers (ABPs) and that passenger seating is in accordance with the aircraft mass and balance requirements.
- Monitor and assist with placing of passenger baggage in approved stowage to ensure this is securely and safely stowed.
- Distribute and monitor use of passenger safety equipment such as infant seatbelts and child restraint devices.
- Give safety briefing to passengers seated at self-help exits.
- Monitor visible aircraft surfaces and advise flight crew of any surface contamination (such as ice or snow).
- Close doors and arm evacuation devices (if installed) in accordance with operator procedures.

Unit 4 Before Take-off
（起飞前）

Section One   Listening

Phrases in Listening

safety demonstration 安全示范   assigned seat 指定位置
safety instruction card 安全须知卡   laptop 手提电脑

Ⅰ. **Watch the video entitled Before Take-off and then discuss the following questions with your partner:**

1. Why is safety demonstration so important?
2. What safety matters will the passengers be reminded of?

Ⅱ. **Listen to the cabin crew's instructions and fill in the missing phrases.**

1. Hello, there, this is the exit row. Have you read the _____ carefully?
2. Excuse me, sir. This is the crew seat. Would you please return to your _____?
3. Hello, sir, this is an _____, so no bags are allowed on the floor. Would you mind putting your bag in the overhead locker for take-off?
4. Can you pull up _____, please, before take-off?
5. Could you please stow your _____?
6. Could you put your seat into the _____, please?
7. Madam, we're preparing for take-off, so can you _____, please?
8. Sir, could you please turn off the _____?
9. Sorry, you'll have to switch off your _____ during take-off or landing.
10. May I help you hang up your coat _____?

Section Two   Conversations

PAX: Passenger   P1: Passenger 1   P2: Passenger 2   P3: Passenger 3   CA: Cabin Attendant

Dialogue 1   Emergency Exit Briefing

CA: Excuse me, Madam, you are sitting near to the emergency exit. According to Civil Aviation Administration of China regulations, you are required to read this safety instruction leaflet carefully. Please do not touch the exit control handle except in an emergency. If this takes place, please help us open the emergency exit and help the passengers evacuate the aircraft. If you have any questions, please let us know. Are you happy to sit here?

PAX: All right. No problem.

Dialogue 2   No Smoking in the Cabin

CA: Excuse me, Sir. Please extinguish your cigarette immediately. This is a non-smoking flight and all toilets are equipped with smoke detectors. Please refrain from smoking during the whole flight.

PAX: This is my first flight and I am a little nervous.

CA: According to regulations, smoking is forbidden on this flight. For the sake of safety, please observe our regulations. We can offer you some sweets or chewing gum to help you relax.

PAX: All right. I appreciate it.

Dialogue 3   Not Using Electronic Devices

CA: (to a passenger who is talking on a mobile phone)
Excuse me, Miss. Please switch off the mobile phone immediately. We are about to take off.

P1: But I am talking to my company CEO. It's urgent. Just a minute, OK?

CA: I am afraid any telephone calls on board the aircraft are strictly prohibited, especially during taxiing and takeoffs, because it will interfere with our navigation and communication system. It is extremely dangerous. Or you can set it to the flying mode.

P1: All right, I'll switch it off soon.

CA: (to another passenger)
Sir, would you please stop using your laptop? The plane will take off soon.

P2: Then, do you mean I can use my computer after take-off?

CA: Yes, but it cannot be switched on until 15 minutes after take-off, and it must be switched off when the seat belt signs come on during the landing time.

P2: OK, I see. Can I have access to internet during the flight?

CA: Yes, you can get access to the Internet. We have WIFI on board.

P2: Got it. Thanks.

CA: Thank you for your understanding.

Dialogue 4   No Using Lavatories

CA: Excuse me, Miss. We'll be taking off soon. You can't stand in the aisle. Please return to your seat and fasten your seatbelt.

PAX: But I have to go to the lavatory.

CA: For the sake of safety, the lavatories have to be closed prior to taking off. Have you noticed that the light is on?

PAX: What does that mean?

CA: It means the use of lavatories has been suspended. You have to wait until the plane comes to a complete standstill. When the seat belt sign turns off, you are free to go to the lavatory.

PAX: All right then.

Dialogue 5　Cabin Facilities

P1: Sir, can you tell me how to return the seat back to the upright position?

CA: Oh, yes. There is a button here on your armrest. Just push it and lean forward at the same time. It will return automatically.

P2: Excuse me, Sir. Where is the reading light?

CA: This is the reading light switch. If you want to read the newspaper, you may turn it on when our plane reaches the cruising altitude. It should be switched off during takeoff and landing.

P3: Could you please tell me how to adjust the air flow/ventilator?

CA: You can turn the knob here in any direction you like. If you want to shut it off, you just turn it tightly to the right.

P3: Thank you for showing me.

CA: You are welcome.

Words in the Conversation

nearby [ˌnɪəˈbaɪ] a. 在附近的	regulation [ˌregjuˈleɪʃn] n. 规则，规章
require [rɪˈkwaɪə(r)] v. 要求	leaflet [ˈliːflət] n. 传单
touch [tʌtʃ] v. 触摸	command [kəˈmɑːnd] v. 命令；指挥
evacuate [ɪˈvækjueɪt] v. 疏散；撤离	urgent [ˈɜːdʒənt] a. 紧急的
notice [ˈnəʊtɪs] v. 注意	standstill [ˈstændstɪl] n. 停止
automatically [ˌɔːtəˈmætɪklɪ] adv. 自动地	ventilator [ˈventɪleɪtə(r)] n. 通风口
forbid [fəˈbɪd] v. 禁止	chew [tʃuː] v. 咀嚼

Useful Expressions

emergency exit 紧急出口　　　　　　　　　CAAC 中国民航总局

Safety Instruction 安全须知　　　　　　　　control handle 控制手柄

refrain from 制止；抑制
chewing gum 口香糖
interfere with 干扰
laptop computer 便携式电脑
navigation and communication system 导航和通讯系统
cruising altitude 巡航高度
electronic device 电子设备

for the sake of 为了…
mobile phone 移动电话
flying mode 飞行模式
seat belt sign 座椅安全带指示灯
get access to 获得；可使用
air flow 气流

Notes

1. We are about to take off. 我们马上就要出发。

   be about to do sth. 表示打算或安排即将发生的动作，它通常不与时间状语连用。如：I was about to go out when someone knocked at the door. 我正要出去，这时有人敲门。

2. We'll be taking off soon. 我们马上就要起飞。

   此处用的将来进行时，主要表示将来某一时间正在进行的动作，常用的时间状语有 soon，this evening，on Sunday，by this time tomorrow，in two days 等等。它表示的是一种客观的制约约束，而不是主观意愿。如：By this time tomorrow, I'll be sitting in the classroom and writing papers.

3. Would you please do sth.? 请你做某事好吗？

   正常情况下，主要用于口语和非正式文体，用来很客气地请求别人帮助。一般所求之事比较容易。

   Would you mind doing sth.? 你介意做某事吗？

   经常用于比较正式的场合，语气非常客气、委婉，或者提醒警告等。所涉及之事难度比较大或会给对方带来不便，或让对方不乐意。

Section Three Language Practice

Ⅰ. Substitution Drills

Read the following sentences and do the same orally with given phrases.

1. For the sake of safety, please ***observe our regulations***.

   a. turn off your mobile phone immediately

   b. extinguish your cigarette right away

   c. stop using electronic devices

   d. fasten your seatbelt and pull up the sunshade

2. You have to wait until ***the plane comes to a complete standstill***.

   a. we reach our cruising altitude

   b. our plane stops climbing

   c. the fasten seatbelt sign is off

   d. we begin to serve meals

3. Thank you for *showing me*.
   a. sharing the information with me
   b. doing so much for me
   c. adjusting the airflow for me
   d. arranging a suitable seat for me

II. **Quick responses**

Look at the model and make quick and proper responses to the following inquiries.

Model: Purser: May I see your documents, please?
       CA: Sure. Here they are.

1. CA: Please refrain from smoking during the whole flight.
   PAX: _____

2. PAX: Why can't I use mobile phone on board?
   CA: _____

3. PAX: Miss, can you tell me how to return the seat back?
   CA: _____

4. PAX: Could you tell me how to use the reading light?
   CA: _____

5. PAX: Could you please tell me how to adjust the air flow?
   CA: _____

III. **Role Play**

1. A passenger is making a telephone call prior to take-off. How do you persuade him to stop making calls?
2. A passenger is smoking in the cabin. How do you stop him?
3. The plane is going to take off. But a passenger wants to go to the lavatory. What would you say to him?
4. A passenger does not know how to return his seat back to the upright position. How do you help him?

IV. **Translate the following sentences into English**

1. 正常情况下请不要去触碰出口处控制手柄。

   _____

2. 紧急情况下，请帮助我们打开紧急出口并指挥乘客撤离飞机。

   _____

3. 请立刻熄灭香烟。

   _____

4. 本次航班禁烟，厕所都安装有烟雾报警器。

   _____

5. 为了安全，请遵守我们的规定。

6. 飞机上严格禁止打电话。

7. 使用电子设备会干扰我们的导航和通讯系统。

8. 飞行期间我可以上网吗？

9. 起飞前厕所关闭。

10. 你能告诉我如何调节通风口吗？

Section Four　Announcements

Safety Demonstration

Ladies and Gentlemen,

We will now explain the use of the life vest, oxygen mask and seatbelt.

Your life vest is located under your seat. To put the vest on, slip it over your head. Secure the straps around your waist and tie them securely.

To inflate the life jacket, pull the tab. Do not inflate it while you are in the cabin. If your life vest is not inflated enough, you can also inflate it manually by blowing into the tube on either side.

Your oxygen mask is in the compartment over your head and it will automatically drop when needed. If you see the mask, pull it towards you firmly to start the flow of oxygen. Place the mask over your nose and mouth, slip the elastic band over your head. Within a few seconds the oxygen flow will begin. Masks are available for children. Please attend your own masks first.

This is your safety belt on your seat. To fasten your seatbelt, insert the link into the main buckle. To be effective, the seatbelt should be fastened tight and low. When you wish to unfasten the seatbelt, lift the flap and pull out the link.

Emergency exits are located on each side of the aircraft. All exits are clearly marked.

Safety Instruction Card in your seat pocket contains additional information. Please read it carefully. Thank you!

Safety Check

Ladies and Gentlemen,

We are ready for departure. Please fasten your seatbelt, open the window shade, put up the tray table, bring your seat back upright and unplug your headphones and electronic devices. The large portable electronic devices, such as laptops, should be stowed properly. Please ensure your cell phones are switched to the airplane mode.

Thank you!

No Smoking

Ladies and Gentlemen,

In accordance with government health regulation, all flights in China are non-smoking. The "No Smoking" sigh will remain switched on throughout the flight. Passengers are also requested to refrain from smoking in the toilets. May we remind you that it is an offence to tamper with the smoke detectors in the toilets?

Your cooperation will be appreciated.

Thank you!

Section Five Interview English

About Academic Records

关于在校成绩

Q1: How were/are your grades/scores at college/university?

你大学的学习成绩如何？

A: They were/are all above average.

They were/are all excellent.

I am ranked second in my class.

My school record was average in my class.

I did quite well. And I achieved the first scholarship twice.

Q2: What was/is your best subject at college?

你大学时哪门课程学的最好？

A: English/Mathematics/Psychology was/is my best subject.

Q3: How many/What foreign languages can you speak?

你会说几门外语？

A: I can speak English well. Besides, I know a little Japanese/Korean/French.

Q4: Which College English Test band did you pass?

你通过了大学英语几级？

A: I passed College English Test Band-4/Band-6.

I passed College English Test Band Six in my third year at college.

Q5: How do you think the education you received at college will contribute to your future work?

你认为你在学校所受到的教育将如何有助于未来的工作？

A: I have learned not only a lot of professional knowledge at college, but also the ability to find out problems and solve them efficiently. In addition, living in the dormitory with my classmates taught me how to get along with others.

As a student majoring in Aviation Service, I learned a lot about how to provide good service to passengers. I think I have a basic understanding of a cabin attendant's work. I hope to be able to make practical use of what I have learned for the benefit of your company.

Section Six Supplementary Vocabulary

taxiing [tæk'siɪŋ] n. 滑行
occupy ['ɒkjupaɪ] v. 使用；占用
latch [lætʃ] v. /n. 闩上/门闩
recline [rɪ'klaɪn] v. 斜倚；倚靠
step aside 让到一边
safety demonstration 安全演示
safety instruction card 安全须知卡

headrest ['hedrest] n. 头靠
remove [rɪ'muːv] v. 拿开；移除
runway ['rʌnweɪ] n. 跑道
footrest ['fʊtrest] n. 脚踏板
ash tray 烟灰缸
seat cushion 坐垫
inaugural flight 试飞，首航

Section Seven Self Study Reading

Before Take-off

Having obtained the approval of the captain, the passengers can be boarded, taken to their seats by the cabin crew, and the process followed is distribution of some products on ground (amenity kit, menus, perfumed napkins, candies, newspapers) and a video and audio presentation of the safety equipment and the evacuation procedures in case of emergency. As soon as the passengers buckle their seatbelts, raise the seat backs, table trays, feet support and sunshades and close the electronic equipment, the cabin crew will transmit to the cabin manager that the entire cabin is ready to take off. Generally speaking, cabin attendants will carry out the following tasks before take-off:

- Conduct a safety demonstration, ensuring all passengers receive this in an appropriate format, with particular regard to SCPs.

- Carry out cabin secure check. This should include seatbelts, seat positions, tables, armrests, footrests, in-flight entertainment systems (IFE), overhead lockers, passenger and crew baggage, exit areas, galleys and equipment including catering supplies, personal electronic devices (PEDs) including mobile phones, and toilets.
- Ensure flight crew are advised that the cabin is secure for take-off.
- Adjust cabin lighting as appropriate.
- Take up their cabin crew stations and fasten seatbelts and harnesses securely.
- Remain alert to potentially hazardous situations.

Unit 5　Beverage Service
（酒水服务）

Section One　Listening

Phrases in Listening

fruit juice 果汁
red wine 红葡萄酒
drinks bar 饮料吧

white wine 白葡萄酒
another Vodka 再来一杯伏特加
mineral water 矿泉水

Ⅰ. Watch the video entitled Beverage Service and discuss the following questions in pairs:
1. What drinks can be available on the flight?
2. Are all the drinks complimentary?

Ⅱ. Listen to the cabin attendant serving drinks to 5 passengers. Put the drinks in the order you hear them ask for.

  a. _____ mineral water
  b. _____ white wine
  c. _____ Sprite
  d. _____ pineapple
  e. _____ Coke

Section Two　Conversations

PAX: Passenger　　CA: Cabin Attendant

Dialogue 1　Juice

CA: Would you like something to drink, Sir?

PAX: Juice, please.

CA: Would you like orange juice, apple juice or tomato juice?

PAX: Tomato.

CA: OK. Would you care for ice?

PAX: No, no ice.

CA: Here you are, Sir.

PAX: That's not enough. I want a full glass.

CA: Shall I leave the can with you?

PAX: Sure.

CA: OK. Enjoy your drink.

Dialogue 2　Tea

CA: Can I offer you a drink, Ma'am?

PAX: Have you got any tea?

CA: Yes, we have black tea, green tea, jasmine tea, peppermint tea and Wulong tea. Which would you like?

PAX: Have you got English Earl Gray tea?

CA: Sorry, I'm afraid not. We have regular black tea.

PAX: OK, that'll be fine. I'd like a cup of black tea, please.

CA: Do you take milk or sugar? Or lemon?

PAX: Milk, please. No sugar. May I have a spoon, please?

CA: No problem. Here you are.

Dialogue 3　Wine

CA: Would you care for something to drink?

PAX: What kind of wine do you have? And where is it made?

CA: We have Great Wall red and white wine. They are made in Yantai with French techniques.
Would you like to have a taste?

PAX: OK. The red wine, please.

CA: On the rocks?

PAX: OK.

PAX: More wine, please.

CA: Sorry, sir. I can't offer you more wine because you may get dehydrated if you drink alcohol. Would you care for some soft drinks, say, green tea?

PAX: OK. Green tea.

Dialogue 4　Drinks Spillage

PAX: Miss, would you care for a drink?

CA: What do you have in your drink cart?

PAX: We are serving tea, coffee, Pepsi Cola, Sprite, Fanta, fruit juice and mineral water.

CA: Sprite, please.

(The CA spills Sprite on the passenger)

CA: I am awfully sorry. Let me help to wipe it up. Do you need another towel?

PAX: Oh, you are so clumsy.

CA: I do apologize, please forgive me. May I offer you some blankets or pillows to cover the wet seat?

PAX: I want to change the seat.

CA: OK. Let me check if there is another seat available in the cabin. Please wait a second.

Dialogue 5 Passenger Comfort

CA: Excuse me, miss. Would you please return your seat back to the upright position so that the gentleman behind you can drink his tea comfortably?

PAX: OK. I have finished my drink.

CA: OK. Can I take it away?

PAX: Thanks.

CA: You are welcome.

Dialogue 6 Sleeping Passenger

PAX: Excuse me, where is my coffee? I have been waiting for a long time. What's up?

CA: Oh, I'm sorry about the delay with your drink. How would you like your coffee, black or white?

PAX: White, please, no sugar.

CA: OK. Here you are. Sorry to have kept you waiting.

PAX: Can you leave another cup of coffee? My husband is sleeping and he will need a drink after he wakes up.

CA: I'm afraid the coffee will spill if there is any sudden turbulence. You may ring the call button for service after she wakes up. And we also have a drinks bar in the galley and he can help hemself to drink there.

PAX: Thanks for the information.

Words in the Conversation

can [kæn] n. 罐头
peppermint ['pepəmɪnt] n. 薄荷
dehydrate [diːˈhaɪdreɪt] v. 脱水
towel [ˈtaʊəl] n. 毛巾
forgive [fəˈɡɪv] v. 原谅
available [əˈveɪləbl] a. 可获得的
turbulence [ˈtɜːbjələns] n. 颠簸
sugar [ˈʃʊɡə(r)] n. 食糖

jasmine [ˈdʒæzmɪn] n. 茉莉花
technique [tekˈniːk] n. 技术
Sprite [spraɪt] n. 雪碧
clumsy [ˈklʌmzi] a. 笨拙的
blanket [ˈblæŋkɪt] n. 毛毯
spill [spɪl] v. 溢出
spillage [ˈspɪlɪdʒ] n. 溢出

Useful Expressions

care for 喜欢

green tea 绿茶

English Earl Grey tea 英国伯爵茶

drink cart 饮料车

ring the call button 按呼叫按钮

black tea 红茶

Wulong tea 乌龙茶

Great Wall red 长城红酒

drinks bar 饮料吧

help oneself 自取；自用

Notes

1. cup 通常指带柄的瓷杯，用来喝茶、牛奶、咖啡等。如：Please pass me a cup of tea.
   glass 通常指玻璃杯，用以饮酒、喝水等。如：Would you like a glass of beer?
   a can of 和 a tin of 意思相同，都表示一罐，一听。如：
   一听可乐 a tin of Coke/a can of Coke.
   a pot of 和 a jar of 表示一罐，或者一壶。如：a pot of coffee 一壶咖啡；a jar of jam 一罐果酱；a jar of honey 一罐蜂蜜；a jar of water 一罐水；a carton of milk 一（纸）盒牛奶。

2. on the rocks，意为加冰块，相当于 with ice。

3. 飞机上的基本饮品有 5 种类，包含果汁（apple juice, orange juice, tomato juice 等）、酒类（beer, wine, liquor, mixed drinks 等）、茶（green tea, black tea, herbal tea, milk tea, lemon tea）、咖啡（instant coffee, percolated coffee）与软性饮料（不含酒精）（cococola, Pepsi, Sprite, Fanta 等）。
   liquors 又为 spirits 烈性酒，可大致分为：
   whisky 威士忌，例如 Scotch Whisky 是烈性酒。品牌：Chivas Regal, Johnny Walker Black Label, Cutty Sark, Old Parr, Johnny Walker Red Label 等；
   brandy 白兰地，品牌：Armagnac 等；
   vodka 伏特加，品牌：Smirnoff, Absolut 等；
   rum 朗姆酒，烈性酒，常用作制作鸡尾酒，类别：Silver Rum, Golden Rum, Dark Rum 等；
   gin 金酒，又称杜松子酒，常用于制作鸡尾酒，类别：Dutch Gin, Dry Gin；
   tequila 龙舌兰酒，品牌有：Cuervo, Ole, Ei Toro 等；
   mixed drinks 混合饮料，鸡尾酒（cocktail），例如，"gin and tonic"，"rum and coke"，"vodka and soda" 都是鸡尾酒。

Section Three Language Practice

I. Substitution Drills

Read the following sentences and do the same orally with given phrases.

1. Would you like *orange juice, apple juice or tomato juice*?
   a. green tea, black tea, herbal tea, milk tea or lemon tea

b. Coke, Pepsi, Sprite or Fanta

　　c. bitter lemon, soda water or tonic water

　　d. Whisky, Brandy, Vodka, Rum, Gin or Tequila

2. I'd like *a cup of Black tea*.

　　a. a can of Coca Cola

　　b. a carton of milk

　　c. a glass of water

　　d. a bottle of mineral water

3. How would you like your *coffee, black or white*?

　　a. tea, weak or strong

　　b. whisky, straight or on the rocks

　　c. coffee, regular or decaffeinated

　　d. water, still or sparking

II. Drinks or drink-related words. Tick the correct column.

NO.	Items	Cold/soft Drink	Hot Drink	Alcohol	Way of Serving
1	beer				
2	Bloody Mary				
3	Pepsi Cola				
4	gin and tonic				
5	juice(apple,orange,tomato,etc.)				
6	no ice				
7	on the rocks/with ice				
8	red wine				
9	sparkling water				
10	soda water				
11	tea(black,green,herbal,etc.)				
12	whisky				
13	vodka				
14	brandy				
15	champagne				

续表

NO.	Items	Cold/soft Drink	Hot Drink	Alcohol	Way of Serving
16	white(tea/coffee)				
17	with milk and sugar				
18	straight				
19	mixed				
20	bourbon				
21	tequila				
22	black label				
23	chivas				
24	cocktail				
25	ginger ale				
26	hot chocolate				

Ⅲ. **Role Play**

1. A passenger inquiries about what kind of wine you have on board. Give her the information.
2. A passenger took a nap and missed the beverage service. After she wakes up, she wants to order her drinks. You give her your advice.
3. You spilt milk on a passenger. You said sorry for what happened and offered a dry towel and a blanket to the passenger.

Ⅳ. **Translate the following sentences into English**

1. 先生，您想喝点什么吗？

2. 我们有红茶、绿茶、茉莉花茶、薄荷茶和乌龙茶。

3. 我想要一杯红茶。

4. 您想喝些软饮料吗，比如绿茶？

5. 我可以给您一些毛毯或者枕头盖在湿掉的椅子上吗？

6. 我来查一下客舱是否还有空位。
   _____

7. 您能将座椅靠背调直让你后面的先生喝茶时可以舒服一些。
   _____

8. 很抱歉没能及时送上饮料。
   _____

9. 您的咖啡是加奶还是不加奶？
   _____

10. 我恐怕突然颠簸时咖啡会溢出来。
    _____

Section Four Announcements

Serving Drinks Before Meal

Ladies and Gentlemen,

　　Now we are going to serve refreshments. We shall be serving tea, coffee, Coke, Sprite, orange juice and mineral water in a moment. You are welcome to take your choice.

　　Thank you!

Sale of Beverage

Ladies and Gentlemen,

　　We will begin our beverage service shortly, followed by dinner. Whisky and brandy at 20 US dollars are available for purchase in the main cabin.

　　Thank you!

Section Five Interview English

About Campus Life
关于校园生活

Q1: Did you get any honors or rewards at college/university?
　　你在大学曾经获得什么荣誉或者奖励吗？

A: Yes. I got the college scholarship three times and was chosen as Merit Student （三好学生）

twice. /Excellent League Member（优秀团员）/Excellent Student Cadre（优秀学生干部）

Yes. I won the first/second/third prize in the Oral English Contest in 2012.

Q2: Did you take any leading position in college?

你在大学期间担任过学生干部吗？

A: Yes. I was the monitor of my class.

I was the president of the Student Union（学生会主席）in our department.

Q3: Did you take part in any club activities in college?

你在大学参加过什么社团活动吗？

A: Yes. I was in the chess club for three years.

I was a member of photography club for two years.

I was a violin player in the college orchestra（管弦乐队）.

Q4: What did you usually do after class when you were in college?

大学时课后你经常做些什么？

A: I usually went swimming in summer and went jogging in winter.

I sometimes played basketball with my roommates and sometimes did some reading in the library.

Q4: Did you enjoy your college life? Why or why not?

你喜欢大学生活吗？为什么？

A: Of course, I did. I enjoyed many things in college. College life gave me a sense of responsibility. Everything I did had to be my own decision. And my parents didn't need to worry about me. Yes, I did. College life not only broadened my knowledge, but also deepened my mind and improved my abilities and gave me the chance to make friends with people from different backgrounds.

Section Six Supplementary Vocabulary

beverage [ˈbevərɪdʒ] n. 饮料	refreshment [rɪˈfreʃmənt] n. 茶点
cocktail [ˈkɒkteɪl] n. 鸡尾酒	alcoholic [ˌælkəˈhɒlɪk] a. 含有酒精的
whisky [ˈwɪski] n. 威士忌	champagne [ʃæmˈpeɪn] n. 香槟
brandy [ˈbrændi] n. 白兰地	rum [rʌm] n. 朗姆酒
gin [dʒɪn] n. 杜松子酒	tequila [təˈkiːlə] n. 龙舌兰酒
bourbon [ˈbɜːbən] n. 波旁威士忌	vodka [ˈvɒdkə] n. 伏特加
straight [streɪt] a. 纯的；不掺水的	Chivas [ʃiːvəs] n. 芝华士酒
soda water 苏打水	tonic water 汤尼水
herbal tea 凉茶	on the rocks 加冰块

> regular coffee 黑咖啡　　　decaffeinated coffee 低因咖啡
> still water 纯净水　　　　sparkling water 气泡水
> black label 黑方（威士忌）　ginger ale 姜汁无酒精饮料

Section Seven　Self Study Reading

Beverage Service

　　Beverage options and product availability may vary by flight. All flights accept credit and debit cards only. Some airlines recycle aluminum cans, newspapers and plastic bottles on eligible flights.

Non-alcoholic beverages

The following complimentary beverages are available on most flights:
- Coca-Cola
- Sprite
- Lime Sparkling Water
- Bottled Water
- Apple Juice, Cranberry Apple Juice Cocktail, Orange Juice, Tomato Juice
- Bloody Mary Mix
- Ginger Ale, Seltzer Water, Tonic Water
- Illy Dark Roast coffee (regular and decaffeinated)
- Hot tea

Alcoholic beverages

　　Alcoholic beverage selections vary by flight and cabin. Only alcoholic beverages served by a flight attendant may be consumed on board. Customers must be 21 or older to consume alcohol.

Beer

- Miller
- Heineken
- Shiner Bock

Specialty cocktails

- Mai Tai
- Cocktails Moscow Mule

House red and white wines

- Redwood Vineyards Cabernet Sauvignon
- Lamoure Roi Chardonnay Vin de France

Spirits

- Tito's Handmade Vodka
- Superior Rum
- Whisky

Unit 6 Meal Service
（餐食服务）

Section One Listening

Phrases in Listening

Muslim Meal 穆斯林餐
run out of 没有…
pure water 纯净水
children' meal 儿童餐
ordinary food 普通餐

Kosher Meal 犹太餐
ice cubes 冰块
special meal 特殊餐食
be mixed with 与…混合
room temperature water 常温水

Ⅰ. Watch the video entitled Meal Service on Board and then discuss the following questions with your partner:
1. What meals could the passengers order?
2. Were the passengers satisfied with the meal service?

Ⅱ. Listen to the dialogue and decide whether the statement is true (T) or False (F).
(   ) 1. Mr. Brown ordered a Kosher Meal.
(   ) 2. The cabin attendant served room temperature water instead of the cold water at last.
(   ) 3. The ice cubes were out of stock on the flight.
(   ) 4. Mr. Brown ordered the children's meal in advance.
(   ) 5. The cabin attendant didn't prepare the children's meal.

Section Two Conversations

PAX: Passenger   CA: Cabin Attendant

Dialogue 1 Main Dish for First Class

CA: Miss. Smith, we'll be serving dinner soon. You can choose between Kung Pao chicken rice and beef noodles. Both are served with mashed potatoes and beans. Which would you prefer?

PAX: Beef noodles, please.

CA: OK. Would you like to have the fruit before or after the meal?

PAX: After the meal.

CA: OK. Miss Smith, we have fruit juice, cola, coffee and red and white wine today. Which one would you like?

PAX: Red wine.

CA: OK. Miss Smith, do you have a special diet?

PAX: Oh, I am allergic to seafood.

CA: OK, I got it. Then you have ordered beef noodles, served with mashed potatoes and beans, fruit after and red wine. Is that right?

PAX: That's right.

CA: The dinner will be ready in 5 minutes. Please wait a moment.

PAX: No problem. Take your time.

CA: Thanks.

Dialogue 2　Main Dish for Economy Class

CA: Excuse me, Sir. Can you set your table? We are serving the dinner.

PAX: What's the main dish today?

CA: For main dishes we have beef noodles and seafood rice. Which one would you prefer?

PAX: Seafood rice, please.

CA: Okay, here you are. What would you like to drink with your meal, Sir?

PAX: A glass of red wine, please.

CA: OK.

PAX: Is it French?

CA: No, it's made in China. It's very nice. Would you like to try it?

PAX: OK.

CA: Here it is. Enjoy your meal.

Dialogue 3　No Seafood Rice

PAX: Can I have the seafood rice?

CA: I'm sorry, we are out of seafood rice, but we still have chicken noodles. It's also delicious. Would you like to try the noodles instead?

PAX: Okay, I will try it. Can I have more napkins?

CA: Of course, Miss. Here you are.

Dialogue 4　Special Meal

PAX: Excuse me, do you have Vegetarian Meals on board?

CA: Did you order it in advance?

PAX: I don't think so.

CA: Let me check, ... I am sorry, there are no more Vegetarian Meals left. Since you didn't order it in advance, and the spare ones have all been served, may I give you more vegetable salad and bread instead?

PAX: Okay, that'll be fine. By the way, what special meals can passengers choose from?

CA: Our passengers have a choice of Hindu Meal, Muslim Meal, Kosher Meal, Baby Meal, Child Meal and Vegetarian Meals. We also offer medical meals to passengers who have special diet requirements. For more information, please go to our official website.

PAX: Thanks a lot.

CA: My pleasure.

Dialogue 5　Children Meal

PAX: Do you have Children's Meals on board?

CA: We do carry preordered special Child Meals for passengers who have booked prior to their flight. Did you book them?

PAX: No, I'm afraid I didn't.

CA: Well, I could check to see if we have any spare meals for you. Would you like me to do that?

PAX: Oh, yes, please. That would be great.

CA: I'll be back in a moment. ... I've got two Children Meals here. It's burger and french fries. Would your children like this fun food?

PAX: Oh, it's their favorite food! Thanks a lot.

CA: You are very welcome.

Dialogue 6　Warming Milk for Baby

PAX: Miss, can you do me a favor?

CA: Certainly. What can I do for you?

PAX: Would you please warm some milk for my baby?

CA: Sure. ... (a few minutes later) Is this warm enough?

PAX: Okay. It is fine.

CA: If there is anything else we can do for you, just press the call button, we are happy to serve you. And if you need to go to the lavatory, just tell me and I will hold the baby for you.

PAX: That'll be great. Thank you.

CA: That's my duty.

Words in the Conversation

serve [sɜːv] v. 服务　　　　　　　　bean [biːn] n. 豆

diet ['daɪət] n. 日常饮食　　　　　allergic [ə'lɜːdʒɪk] n. 过敏的

seafood ['siːfuːd] n. 海鲜
napkin ['næpkɪn] n. 餐巾纸
spare [speə(r)] a. 备用的
website ['websaɪt] n. 网站
mash [mæʃ] v. 捣碎
vegetarian [ˌvedʒə'teəriən] a. 素食的
official [ə'fɪʃl] a. 正式的
favor ['feɪvə] n. 欢心；好感

Useful Expressions

Kung Pao chicken 宫保鸡丁
fruit before or after the meal 餐前上水果还是餐后上水果
have a special diet 有忌口
set the table 摆桌子（准备吃饭）
main dish 主菜
Hindu Meal 印度餐
special diet requirement 特殊饮食需求
preordered meal 预订的餐食
spare meal 备用餐食

mashed potatoes 土豆泥
be allergic to seafood 对海鲜过敏
seafood rice 海鲜饭
in advance 提前
baby meal 婴儿餐
official website 官方网站
prior to 在…之前
warm some milk 热点牛奶

Notes

Inflight Special Meals 机上特殊餐食及代码（仅供参考）

Code	English	Chinese	Code	English	Chinese
HNML	Hindu Meal	印度餐	DBML	Diabetic Meal	糖尿病患者餐
KSML	Kosher Meal	犹太餐	PRML	Purine Meal	低嘌呤餐
JAIN	Jain Menu	耆那餐	GFML	Gluten Free Meal	无面筋餐
MOML	Moslem Meal	穆斯林餐、清真餐	BLML	Bland Meal	低纤维餐
A, VGML	Asian Vegetarian Meal	亚洲素食	HFML	High Fiber Meal	高纤维餐
I, VGML	Indian Vegetarian Meal	印度素食	LCML	Low Calorie Meal	低热量餐
O, VGML	Oriental Vegetarian Meal	东方素食	LFML	Low Cholesterol Meal	低胆固醇餐
W, VGML	Western Vegetarian Meal	西方素食	LPML	Low Protein Meal	低蛋白质餐
VGML	Vegan Vegetarian Meal	纯素食(不含蛋、奶)	LSML	Low Sodium Meal	无盐餐
VLML	Vegetarian Meal	素食(含蛋、奶)	NLML	Non Lactose Meal	无乳糖餐
RVML	Raw Vegetarian Meal	果蔬餐			
SFML	Seafood Meal	海味餐			
FPML	Fruit Platter Meal	水果餐			
BBML	Baby Meal	婴儿餐			
CHML	Child Meal	儿童餐			

Section Three   Language Practice

Ⅰ. **Substitution Drills**

Read the following sentences and do the same orally with the given phrases.

1. We'll be serving **dinner** soon. You can choose between **Kung Pao chicken rice and beef noodles**.

    a. breakfast—roast beef and chicken

    b. lunch— pork with rice and fish with noodles

    c. desert—pudding and ice cream

    d. dinner—beef with mushroom source and poached salmon

2. I'm sorry, we are out of **the seafood rice**, but we still have **chicken noodles**.

    a. fruit salad—vegetable salad

    b. French dressing—Thailand dressing

    c. beef rice—fish noodles

    d. vanilla ice cream —strawberry ice cream

3. I am sorry, there are no more **Vegetarian Meal** left. May I give you more **vegetable salad and bread** instead?

    a. vegetable salad—fruit salad

    b. mushroom source—tomato source

    c. gateau—mousse

    d. garlic bread—bean paste bread

Ⅱ. **Read the special meals in the box and match the names in column A with the explanations in column B.**

There are many types of special meals for passengers as well as cabin crew.		
Medical Meals	**Cultural Meals**	**Other Special Meals**
Bland	Chinese, Indian, Japanese, etc.	Children
Diabetic		Infant and Baby
Gluten-free	**Religious Meals**	Vegan
Low fat	Hindu	Vegetarian
Low cholesterol	Buddhist and Jain	
Low salt	Halal	
Low calorie	Kosher	
High fiber	Muslim	
Non lactose		
Peanut free		

A	B
1. Hindu	a. It is fun food for kids.
2. Muslim	b. It is for those who need to keep blood sugar level.
3. Child	c. The food does not contain beef.
4. Diabetic	d. The meal is low in fat and sugar.
5. Low calorie	e. The meal has no pork or by-products of pork.

Ⅲ. **Role Play**
1. A passenger wants to know today's main dish. How do you respond?
2. A passenger wants to have vegetarian meal on board but he didn't order it in advance. How will you handle this situation?
3. A passenger asks for seafood rice but it is out of stock. What will you do?

Ⅳ. **Translate the following sentences into English**
1. 水果您是餐前吃还是餐后吃?

2. 晚餐5分钟之后就好。请稍等。

3. 先生,您能把小桌板放好吗?我们很快就供应晚餐了。

4. 我们的主食有牛肉面和海鲜饭,您想要哪一种?

5. 抱歉,海鲜饭没有了,但是我们还有鸡肉面。

6. 飞机上有素食餐吗?

7. 想要了解更多信息请前往我们的官方网站。

8. 我会确认一下是否有备用餐食。

9. 我们的乘客可以选择印度餐、穆斯林餐、犹太餐、婴儿餐、儿童餐和素食餐。

10. 你能为我的孩子热些牛奶吗？

Section Four　Announcements

Meal Service

Ladies and Gentlemen,
　　Our aircraft has left Shanghai. We are going to provide you with a beverage and breakfast service shortly.

Before Dinner

Ladies and Gentlemen,
　　We will soon be serving dinner. We are offering you a choice of noodles with chicken and rice with beef. We have also prepared a Muslim and a Vegetarian Meal. If you have special diet requirements, please tell the flight attendant.
　　Thank you!

Meal Order

Ladies and Gentlemen,
　　We are now beginning to take meal orders. Today we have prepared you a selection of hot meals for only 10 yuan. If you would like to order a meal, please press the call button or just ask one of our cabin crews.
　　Thank you!

Section Five　Interview English

About Your Part-time Job
关于业余工作

Q1：Did you ever do a part time job in college?

你在大学时曾做过什么兼职工作？

A: Yes. I worked as a waiter at KFC/Starbucks in my second year at college.

Yes. I served as a secretary, salesgirl, surveyor for a company.

Yes. I used to work as a tutor for pupils in primary schools.

Q2: Why were you engaged in a part-time job?

你为什么想到做一份兼职工作？

A: I wanted to enrich my experience and broaden my horizons.

Frankly speaking, I need a part-time job to earn some money so as to afford my tuition.

I think I can learn how to communicate with different people by doing a part-time job.

Q3: How did you spend the money earned from your part-time job?

你兼职工作的钱作何用处？

A: I spent the money on paying for my tuition.

I like traveling, so I saved the money up for that reason.

I posted some of the money to my parents to help them to support the family and used the spare money to help with my living expenses.

Q4: How did you get along with your colleagues?

你与同事们相处得如何？

A: I got along well with my colleagues. I am a girl and I like to make friends.

Very well. I enjoy working with all my colleagues.

Q5: What have you learned from your part-time job?

你从兼职工作中学到了什么？

A: I have learned many things. I realized the meaning of responsibility. I also gained a lot of experience in serving customers.

I have learned how to deal with different clients.

I have gained experience in teaching small children.

Section Six Supplementary Vocabulary

snack [snæk] n. 快餐，小吃

delicacy ['delɪkəsi] n. 美食

sandwich ['sænwɪtʃ] n. 三明治

appetizers ['æpɪtaɪzə(r)] n. 开胃品

dietary ['daɪətəri] n. 饮食的

dessert [dɪ'zɜːt] n. 餐后甜点

sauce [sɔːs] n. 调味汁、酱料

reservation [ˌrezə'veɪʃn] n. 预订

vegan ['viːɡən] n. 严格的素食主义者

spicy ['spaɪsi] a. 辛辣的

bland [blænd] *a.* 清淡的
gateau ['gætəʊ] *n.* 奶油蛋糕
cuisine [kwɪ'ziːn] *n.* 菜肴；烹饪
vanilla ice cream 香草冰激凌
garlic bread 蒜蓉面包
catering company 配餐公司
meal tray 餐盘

gluten ['gluːtn] *n.* 麦麸
mousse [muːs] *n.* 慕斯
speciality [ˌspeʃi'æləti] *n.* 特产
strawberry ice cream 草莓冰激凌
bean paste bread 豆沙面包
drink trolley 饮料推车

Section Seven Self Study Reading

Meal Service

An airline meal, airline food, plane food or in-flight meal is a meal served to passengers on board a commercial airliner. These meals are prepared by specialist airline catering services and normally served to passengers using an airline service trolley.

These meals vary widely in quality and quantity across different airline companies and classes of travel. They range from a simple snack or beverage in short-haul Economy Class to a seven-course gourmet meal in a First Class long haul flight. When ticket prices were regulated in the American domestic market, food was the primary means airlines differentiated themselves.

The first airline meals were served by Handley Page Transport, an airline company founded in 1919, to serve the London-Paris route in October of that year. Passengers could choose from a selection of sandwiches and fruit.

The type of food varies depending upon the airline company and class of travel. Meals may be served on one tray or in multiple courses with no tray and with a tablecloth, metal cutlery and glassware (generally in First and Business Classes). Often the food is reflective of the culture of the country the airline is based in.

The airline dinner typically includes meat (most commonly chicken or beef), fish or pasta, a salad or vegetable, a small bread roll and a dessert. Condiments (typically salt, pepper and sugar) are supplied in small sachets or shakers.

Caterers usually produce alternative meals for passengers with restrieted diets. These must usually be ordered in advance, sometimes when buying the ticket. Some of the more common examples include:

Cultural diets, such as Turkish, French, Italian, Chinese, Korean, Japanese and Indian style.

Infant and baby meals. Some airlines also offer children's meals, containing food that children will enjoy such as baked beans, mini hamburgers and hot dogs.

Medical diets, including low/high fiber, low fat/cholesterol, diabetic, peanut free, non-lactose, low salt/sodium, low-purine, low calorie, low protein, bland (non spicy) and gluten-free meals.

Religious diets, including Kosher, Halal and Hindu, Buddhist and Jain Vegetarian (sometimes termed Asian Vegetarian) Meals.

Vegetarian and vegan meals. Some airlines do not offer a specific meal for non vegan vegetarians; instead, they are given a vegan meal.

Unit 7 Entertainment Service
（娱乐服务）

Section One Listening

Phrases in Listening

in-flight entertainment 机上娱乐
long-haul flight 长途航班
medium-haul aircraft 中程航班
TV series 电视连续剧
user interface 用户界面

It guarantees you… 保证你…
entertainment app 娱乐软件
current blockbuster 热映大片
audio book 有声书
modern tablet 现代平板电脑

Ⅰ. Watch the video entitled Entertainment service and discuss the following questions in pairs:

1. What channels are available for you to choose from?
2. What would you like to do if you want to relax for a while on the flight?

Ⅱ. Listen to the advertisement of the airlines and fill in the missing numbers.

1. _____ films in up to eight languages.
2. _____ TV programs.
3. Large selection for families and children with many movies and TV programs, _____ Audio books and Music CDs.
4. _____ "Box Sets" to enjoy featuring whole seasons of _____ TV series.
5. _____ Lufthansa Playlists to relax and to tune in for many destinations.
6. A big selection of _____ Music CDs with an excellent selection of Rock，Pop，Classical and among them _____ is soft music.
7. _____ Audio Books in German and English.
8. _____ International programs, including _____ contents from the Middle East，India，Japan and China.
9. Simple operation：the user interface can be operated in the same way as modern tablet interfaces and is available in _____ languages.

Section Two Conversations

PAX: Passenger   CA: Cabin Attendant

Dialogue 1   Something to Read

PAX: Excuse me, can I have something to read?

CA: Of course. We have CAAC in flight magazines and some local newspapers. Which would you like?

PAX: Give me a copy of in-flight magazine, please.

CA: Here it is. It is in the seat pocket in front of you.

PAX: Thanks. By the way, are there any English newspapers or magazines available on board?

CA: Sure. For English newspapers, today we have *China Daily Overseas* and *Shanghai Daily* and for English magazines, we have *Times* and *National Geographic*. Which one would you like to read?

PAX: *National Geographic*, please.

CA: OK, here you are.

Dialogue 2   Changing Headset

PAX: Miss, can I have a headset?

CA: It's in the seat pocket in front of you.

PAX: Oh, thanks.... But it is not working. Can I get a new one?

CA: All right! Please wait a moment. I'll get a new one for you.

Dialogue 3   Changing Volume

CA: Did you call, Madam?

PAX: Oh yes, What's the matter with this thing?

CA: Your headset?

PAX: Yes, I don't have any sound.

CA: I'm sorry about that. Please make sure that your headphones are plugged in properly.

PAX: Oh, they are in the right place, just not working.

CA: Let me show you. First, press the volume button here and then press the up and down button. After that, you can enjoy the music.

PAX: Oh, that's it. Thanks a lot.

CA: You are welcome.

Dialogue 4   Searching for Music Channel

PAX: Sorry to bother you, but I need your help.

CA: How can I help you? What's the matter?

PAX: I want to listen to music but I can't find the music channel.

CA: Don't worry, I'll show you. Press "Menu" first, then "Music". See that? What kind of music do you want to listen to?

PAX: Classical music.

CA: OK, so first press "Select", and then "Play". Here it goes. Enjoy the music.

PAX: Thanks a lot.

CA: Don't mention it. It's my duty.

Dialogue 5 Resetting the Screen

PAX: Miss, something is wrong with my entertainment system. You see I have got a blank screen.

CA: Sorry about that. I will reset it for you right away. It will take a couple of minutes. Please don't touch any buttons on the control until I come back.

PAX: OK, Miss.

Dialogue 6 Amenity Kit

PAX: Excuse me, do you have anything for my 4-year-old daughter?

CA: Yes, we do. We have amenity kits for children which contain a story book, coloring book and crayons. I will get one for you. Please wait a moment.

PAX: Oh, that's very considerate of you. Thanks a lot.

CA: You are welcome.

Words in the Conversation

geographic [ˌdʒiə'græfik] adj. 地理的	copy ['kɒpi] n. 一份
headset ['hedset] n. 戴在头上的耳机	volume ['vɒljuːm] n. 音量
stuff [stʌf] n. 东西	headphone ['hedfəun] n. 双耳式耳机
plug [plʌg] v. 插入	properly ['prɒpəli] adv. 适当地
press [pres] v. 按；压	bother ['bɒðə(r)] v. 打扰
channel ['tʃænl] n. 频道	select [sɪ'lekt] v. 选择
screen [skriːn] n. 屏幕	kit [kɪt] n. 装备
crayon ['kreɪən] n. 彩色蜡笔	considerate [kən'sɪdərət] a. 体贴的

Useful Expressions

in-flight magazine 机上杂志   local newspaper 当地报纸
China Daily Overseas《中国日报（海外版）》   *National Geographic*《国家地理》
volume button 音量按钮   classical music 古典音乐

Notes

CAAC 是中国民用航空局的英文缩写，全称为 Civil Aviation Administration of China。

Section Three Language Practice

Ⅰ. **Substitution Drills**

Read the following sentences and do the same orally with the given phrases.

1. Let me show you. First, ***press the volume button here*** and then ***press the up and down button***. After that, ***you can enjoy the music***.

    a. put on the headset—select the movie channel—you can enjoy the movie

    b. press the button on your armrest—select the music channel—you can relax

    c. pull the folded table out—place it in front of you—you can select the channel you like

    d. put the plugs into your ears—put the jack into the hole at the armrest—you can enjoy yourself

2. Please make sure that ***your headphones are plugged in properly***.

    a. your seatbelt is fastened

    b. your footrest is stowed

    c. the reading light is turned off

    d. your baggage is in the overhead locker or under the seat in front of you

3. Please don't ***touch any button on the control*** until ***I come back***.

    a. release your seatbelt—the fasten seatbelt sign is off

    b. move around—we reach the cruising altitude

    c. go to the lavatory—it is 15 minutes after take off

    d. take out the life jacket—you are instructed to do so

Ⅱ. **Quick responses**

Look at the model and make quick and proper responses to the following inquiries.

Model: Purser: May I see your documents, please?

　　　　CA: Sure. Here they are.

1. PAX: Excuse me, Miss. Can I have something to read?
    CA: _____
2. PAX: By the way, are there any English newspapers or magazines available on board?
    CA: _____
3. PAX: Could I get a new pair of headset?
    CA: _____
4. PAX: I want to listen to music but I can't find the music channel.
    CA: _____
5. PAX: Excuse me, Miss, do you have anything for my 5 year old son?
    CA: _____

Ⅲ. **Role Play**

1. A passenger wants to read something on board. What do you recommend?

2. When passengers don't know how to use the headsets to listen to music, how do you instruct them?

3. What do you usually provide for children on board?

Ⅳ. **Translate the following sentences into English**

1. 我们有民航机上杂志和一些地方报纸。您要哪一种？

2. 机上杂志在您前方座椅口袋内。

3. 我的耳机坏了，我可以拿个新的吗？

4. 首先按音量键，然后按上下键。

5. 抱歉打扰您，但是我需要您的帮助。

6. 在我回来之前请不要按面板上的任何按钮。

7. 我的娱乐系统出问题了。

8. 我们有儿童套装，里面有故事书、画画书和蜡笔。

9. 我想听音乐，但是找不到音乐频道。

10. 你考虑得真周到。

Section Four Announcements

Entertainment Service

Ladies and Gentlemen,

　　Now we will be showing in-flight entertainment programs such as film, music and others. We hope you will enjoy them.

　　Please use the headset in the seat pocket in front of you. Choose channel which corresponds with the programs that you wish to watch. You may ask your cabin attendants for assistance.

Section Five Interview English

About Your Personality
关于性格

Q1: What kind of person are you? / How would you describe yourself?

你是怎样类型的人？/ 你怎样形容你自己呢？

A: I am outgoing, friendly, passionate and optimistic.

I am a little shy. I feel nervous when I speak in public. I know I have to overcome this and in fact I am working on it now.

I am a hard-working and responsible person. I never give up and I don't like to leave things half-done.

I am a curious person and I like to learn new things.

Q2: What is your personality?

你认为自己的性格如何？

A: I think I am a little introverted and quiet. I am quite strict with myself. I like to have everything done very well.

I am an extroverted person. I like making friends and talking with them. I am enthusiastic about everything.

I am honest, modest and sincere.

Generally speaking, I'm outgoing and enjoying doing things with others.

Q3: What do your friends think of you?

你在朋友眼中是怎样的？

A: They say that I am honest, and they like me because I am not selfish. They feel very comfortable staying with me.

My friends always say that I am an energetic and active person. They enjoy talking and playing with me.

Q4: Would you tell me your weak points and strong points?

你能谈一谈自己的优缺点吗？

A: As a student just graduated from college, I used to be a little shy in the public. That's perhaps my weak point. But I'm willing to learn from others and I'm patient and responsible.

Section Six Supplementary Vocabulary

documentary [ˌdɒkjuˈmentri] n. 纪录片
jack [dʒæk] n. 插座；插口
souvenir [ˌsuːvəˈnɪə(r)] n. 纪念品
slide [slaɪd] v. 滑动
child packs 儿童玩具包
Passenger Service Unit 旅客服务装置
comedy [ˈkɒmədi] n. 喜剧
reset [ˌriːˈset] v. 重启；重新设置
handle [ˈhændl] v. 处理；应付
drama [ˈdrɑːmə] n. 戏剧
satellite telephone （机上）卫星电话
audio program 音频节目

Section Seven Self Study Reading

In flight entertainment

In-flight entertainment (IFE) refers to the entertainment available to aircraft passengers during a flight. In 1936, the airship Hindenburg offered passengers a piano, lounge, dining room, smoking room and bar during the 2.5 day flight between Europe and America. After the Second World War, IFE was delivered in the form of food and drink services, along with an occasional projector movie during lengthy flights. In 1985, the first personal audio player was offered to passengers, along with noise cancelling headphones in 1989. During the 1990s the demand for better IFE was a major factor in the design of aircraft cabins. Before then, the most a passenger could expect was a movie projected on a screen at the front of a cabin, which could be heard via a headphone socket at his or her seat. Now, in most aircraft, private IFE TV screens are offered on most airlines.

• Moving map systems

A moving map system is a real-time flight information video channel that is broadcast through to cabin project/video screens and personal televisions (PTVs). In addition to displaying a map that illustrates the position and direction of the plane, the system gives the altitude, airspeed, outside air temperature, distance to the destination, distance from the origination point and local time. The moving-map system information is derived in real time from the aircraft's flight computer systems.

• Audio entertainment

Audio entertainment covers music, news, information and comedy. Most music channels are pre-recorded and feature their own DJs to provide chatter, song introductions and interviews with artists. In addition, there is sometimes a channel devoted to the plane's radio communications, allowing passengers to listen in on the pilot's in-flight conversations with other planes and ground stations.

• Video entertainment

Video entertainment is provided via a large video screen at the front of a cabin section, as well as smaller monitors situated every few rows above the aisles. Sound is supplied via the same headphones as those distributed for audio entertainment.

• Video games

Some airlines also provide video games as part of the video entertainment system. For example, Singapore Airlines passengers on some flights have access to a number of

Super Nintendo games as part of its entertainment system. Also, Virgin America's and V Australia's new RED Entertainment System offers passengers Internet gaming over a Linux-based operating system.

• Personal televisions

Some airlines have now installed personal televisions (otherwise known as PTVs) for every passenger on most long-haul routes. These televisions are usually located in the seat backs or tucked away in the armrests for front row seats and First Class. Some airlines show direct broadcast satellite television which enables passengers to view live TV broadcasts. Some airlines also offer video games using PTV equipment. Fewer still provide closed captioning for deaf and hard-of-hearing passengers.

Unit 8 Duty-free Service
（免税商品销售服务）

Section One Listening

Phrases in Listening

duty-free sales 免税销售
by cash 现金支付
classic perfume 经典款香水
cosmetics package 化妆品套装
USD（US dollar）美元
RMB（Renminbi）人民币
JPY（Japanese yen）日元

duty-free catalogue 免税商品目录
by credit card 信用卡支付
quartz watch 石英手表
people's currency 人民币
EUR（Euro）欧元
SGD（Singapore dollar）新加坡元
CAD（Canadian dollar）加拿大元

Ⅰ. Watch the video entitled In-flight Duty-free Sales and discuss the following questions in pairs:
1. Where were these people?
2. Where could the passengers find duty-free sales information?
3. What items did the passenger buy?
4. How did the passenger pay for his order?

Ⅱ. On international flights, you may need to offer duty-free items to passengers. Circle the price you hear for each item.

1. classic perfume   A. 79 USD   B. 49 USD
2. quartz watch   A. 100EUR   B. 900 RMB
3. cosmetics package   A. 302 SGD   B. 320 SGD
4. necklace   A. 8875JPY   B. 8865 JPY
5. chocolate   A. 142CAD   B. 79EUR

Section Two Conversations

PAX: Passenger   CA: Cabin Attendant

Dialogue 1　Inquiring about Duty-free Sales

PAX: Excuse me. Do you sell duty-free items on board?

CA: Yes. You can have a look at our duty-free sale catalogue (DFS) in the seat pocket. You have a choice of liquors, cigarettes, perfumes, cosmetics, chocolates, watches... They are of excellent quality and at a reasonable price.

PAX: Thanks. Could you tell me how many bottles of alcohol I can take into Hong Kong?

CA: One liter of wines or spirits is allowed for non-residents and one liter of wines or spirits for residents.

PAX: Thanks.

CA: I have to remind you that our rates of exchange are company rates, which are not necessarily the current bank rates.

PAX: That'll be fine.

Dialogue 2　Recommending Gifts

CA: Hi, there. Would you like to have a look at our duty-free items? We have a fine selection on board today.

PAX: Well, I'd like to buy a gift for my mother. Could you recommend something?

CA: Sure. How about perfumes or cosmetics?

PAX: Oh, I don't think she will like them.

CA: Our airlines also offer specially designed scarves. They are 100% pure silk. It has been very popular today. Would you take one?

PAX: OK. Thanks.

Dialogue 3　On-line Order

PAX: Excuse me, Miss.

CA: Yes? May I help you?

PAX: I have ordered a watch from your company official online website. When can I have it?

CA: Well, could you show me the order number?

PAX: Here it is.

CA: Wait a moment. I'll get it for you... Here you are.

PAX: Thanks!

Dialogue 4　Means of Payment

CA: Perfumes, gifts, chocolates, alcohol, toys...

PAX: Excuse me?

CA: What can I get for you, Miss?

PAX: I'm looking for a light perfume for my husband's birthday.

CA: I have the perfect one. It is classic, the very best and it is a bargain too, at only 50 dollars.

PAX: OK, I'll take it.

CA: How would you like to pay? By cash or by credit card?

PAX: What kinds of cards do you accept?

CA: Most major credit card or debit cards such as Master Card, Visa Card, American Express are all accepted. Or you can also pay by Alipay.

PAX: OK. By credit card. Here is also my frequent flyer card, for the points.

CA: Thank you. Please sign your name here. Would you like a receipt or just the credit card printout?

PAX: I need the receipt too, please.

CA: No problem. Here is your receipt. Here are your cards and this is your gift.

PAX: Thank you!

Dialogue 5　No Discount

PAX: Miss, I will take all of them. How much is it altogether?

CA: Let me add them up. Oh, it is 280 dollars.

PAX: I have bought so many duty-free items. Could you give me a discount?

CA: I am sorry, we can't give you any discounts. All the items are sold at marked price on the flight.

PAX: OK. Here is the cash, 300 dollars.

CA: OK, here is the change, 20 dollars.

Dialogue 6　Being out of Stock

PAX: I am looking for a bottle of Johnny Walker.

CA: I'm sorry, Sir. This particular item is currently out of stock. It has been sold out. Would you like something else?

PAX: Can you give me some suggestions?

CA: We have got Chivas Regal, Bacardi Rum and Smirnoff Vodka. They are all good quality.

PAX: Okay, I will take Chivas Regal and Vodka.

CA: I'm sorry, Sir, but you are allowed only 1 litre of spirits.

PAX: OK, then. I will also have a small bottle of cologne, Yves St Laurent.

CA: We have that in a 50 ml bottle. Is that OK?

PAX: OK.

CA: That is 16 Euros and 40 Euros. Let me add them up. It will be 56 Euros altogether. Cash or credit card?

PAX: Credit card.

CA: Thanks. Enjoy the rest of your flight.

Words in the Conversation

catalogue [ˈkætəlɒg] n. 目录
liquor [ˈlɪkə(r)] n. 烈性酒
perfume [ˈpɜːfjuːm] n. 香水
reasonable [ˈriːznəbl] a. 合理的
liter [ˈliːtə(r)] n. （容量单位）升
scarf [skɑːf] n. 围巾
cash [kæʃ] n. 现金
discount [ˈdɪskaʊnt] n. 折扣
stock [stɒk] n. 库存
debit [ˈdebɪt] n. 借方

choice [tʃɔɪs] n. 选择
cigarette [ˌsɪgəˈret] n. 香烟
cosmetic [kɒzˈmetɪk] n. 化妆品
alcohol [ˈælkəhɒl] n. 酒精
recommend [ˌrekəˈmend] v. 推荐
bargain [ˈbɑːgən] v. 讨价还价
receipt [rɪˈsiːt] n. 收据
particular [pəˈtɪkjələ(r)] a. 特别的
cologne [kəˈləʊn] n. 古龙水
spirit [ˈspɪrɪt] n. 烈酒

Useful Expressions

duty-free item 免税商品
credit card 信用卡
Master Card 万事达卡
American Express 美国运通卡
Johnny Walker 尊尼获加威士忌
be sold out 卖光；脱销

rate of exchange 汇率
frequent flyer 常旅客
Visa Card 维萨卡
marked price 标价
Alipay 支付宝

Notes

1. sign v. 签名，名词 signature
   Would you please sign your name here?
   Please sign your name.
   Please put your signature here.

2. 各种支付方式
   pay by cash 或者 pay in cash 现金付款
   pay by credit card 信用卡付款
   pay in check 用支票付款
   pay by Alipay 用支付宝付款
   pay by WeChat wallet 用微信钱包支付
   pay by QR code 用二维码支付

Section Three Language Practice

Ⅰ. **Substitution Drills**

Read the following sentences and follow the same pattern orally with the phrases given.

1. I have to remind you that *our rates of exchange are company rates, which are not necessarily the current bank rates.*
   a. we don't accept traveler's checks on board
   b. all the items are sold at marked price on the flight
   c. the exchange rate is not the current bank rate
   d. one passenger is only allowed one liter of spirits

2. This kind of scarves has been very popular today.
   a. this set of cosmetics
   b. this kind of cigarette
   c. this typical Chinese tie
   d. this one with traditional design and color

3. That is **16 Euros** and **40 Euros**. Let me add them up. It will be **56 Euros** altogether.
   a. 45 RMB—25 RMB—70 RMB
   b. 34 USD—10 USD—44 USD
   c. 550 JPY—1022 JPY—1572 JPY
   d. 82 CAD—120CAD—202 CAD

II. Quick responses

Look at the model and make quick and proper responses to the following inquiries.

Model: Purser: May I see your documents, please?
       CA: Sure. Here they are.

1. PAX: Could you tell me how many bottles of alcohol I can take into Hong Kong?
   CA: _____

2. PAX: Where can I get my online order?
   CA: _____

3. PAX: Could you recommend something for my wife?
   CA: _____

4. PAX: What kinds of cards do you accept?
   CA: _____

5. PAX: Could you give me a discount?
   CA: _____

III. Role Play

1. A passenger wants to buy a bottle of vodka but it is out of stock. How do you explain this to the passenger?

2. A passenger asks for your suggestion about his wife's birthday present. What do you recommend?

3. A passenger asks you to give him a discount. What do you say to him?

Ⅳ. **Translate the following sentences into English**

1. 你们飞机上卖免税商品吗?

2. 这些商品质量优良,价格合理。

3. 你能告诉我我可以带多少酒去香港吗?

4. 我想买个礼物给我女朋友。你能推荐一些吗?

5. 我在你们公司官网上订购了一块手表。

6. 我正在为我妻子寻找一款淡香水作为生日礼物。

7. 大多数主要信用卡,如万事达、维萨、美国运通都可以使用。

8. 您想要收据还是只要信用卡小票?

9. 很抱歉,不能给您打折。

10. 这种商品目前没有库存。

Section Four Announcements

Duty-free Sales

Ladies and Gentlemen,

May I have your attention, please?

In order to further meet your traveling needs, we are going to offer you a wide selection of duty-free items. All items on board are priced in US dollars and are sold at marked prices so we can't give you any discounts. Please check with our cabin attendant for prices in other currencies. Most major currencies are accepted for your purchases. The major credit cards are also accepted.

Detailed information can be found in the duty-free catalog in the seat pocket in front of you.

Thank you for your cooperation!

Duty-free Sales

Ladies and Gentlemen,

　　We will soon start duty-free sales. Please refer to the duty-free shopping guide for more details.

　　For passengers who are in transit, please note that Liquid Aerosol and Gel items purchased onboard must be kept in a sealed bag with receipts. Please keep your boarding pass and get items ready for inspection at the security check.

In-flight Shop

Ladies and Gentlemen,

　　Available from our inflight shop is a wide range of perfumes, cosmetics, cigarettes and alcohol. They are all at duty-free prices.

　　We accept US dollar, Euro and Japanese yen. We also accept all major credit cards, such as Master Card, Visa and American Express.

　　Thank you!

Section Five　Interview English

About Your Interests & Hobbies
关于你的兴趣爱好

Q1: What do you do for recreation? / What kind of recreation do you like best?
　　你平时的娱乐活动是什么？/ 你最喜欢的娱乐活动是什么？

A: I like traveling and watching all kinds of movies.

　I sometimes go to the KTV with my friends on weekends.

　I go running or play basketball or do something else to keep fit.

　I usually do some reading, go shopping or go swimming. I also play badminton and tennis with my friends.

Q2: What are your interests / hobbies?
　　你的兴趣/爱好是什么？

A: My interests are collecting coins and stamps.

　I have many hobbies. I like all kinds of sports and I also like listening to all types of music.

　I like reading. I usually spent a lot of time in the library. I read all kinds of novels, articles and travel books.

Q3: What is your favorite sport?

你最爱的运动是什么?

A: My favorite sport is table tennis.

Frankly speaking, I enjoy almost all sports. If I have to choose one of them, definitely football.

Q4: Do you like reading?

你喜欢阅读吗?

A: Yes, I do. I enjoy reading biographies, especially those of well-known scientists and artists. I can learn a lot from their stories.

Yes, I like reading novels. Reading keeps me relaxed after a day's studying.

Section Six　Supplementary Vocabulary

visa ['viːzə] n. 签证
declare [dɪˈkleə(r)] v. 申报
current [ˈkʌrənt] a. 现在的
purchase [ˈpɜːtʃəs] v./n. 购买
confectionery [kənˈfekʃənəri] n. 甜食（糖果、巧克力等）
aerosol [ˈeərəsɒl] n. 喷雾剂
traveler's check 旅行支票
duty-free allowance 免税限额
duty-free article/goods 免税物品

jewelry [ˈdʒuːəlrɪ] n. 珠宝；首饰
tobacco [təˈbækəʊ] n. 烟草
tip [tɪp] n. 小费
aftershave [ˈɑːftəʃeɪv] n. 须后水

gel [dʒel] n. 凝胶
retail price 零售价
customs regulation 海关规定
foreign currency 外币

Section Seven　Self Study Reading

Duty-free Shops

Apart from the duty-free shops in the departure lounge at the airport, cabin attendant also sell a range of duty-free goods on international flights. By shopping duty-free, up to 40% off the suggested retail price can be saved. Passengers can leaf through the in-flight magazines or duty-free catalogues located in the seat pocket in front of them. Passengers can choose from the most popular perfumes, elegant accessories and trendy entertainment electronics. Sometimes they will find the best Swiss chocolate, exclusive watches and well-known beauty products. Some items are by renowned labels and represent high quality, including

- Cigarettes
- Confectionery/chocolates
- Cosmetics

- Electronic good
- Gifts
- Perfumes
- Skincare products
- Jewelry
- Spirits
- Watches

Usually after an announcement, cabin attendants will offer the goods using duty-free goods carts and proceed through the cabin stopping at each row of passengers. The goods can be paid for with cash, such as US $ (dollars), Euros or most major credit cards, such as Diners Club, Visa, Master card, American Express and JCB. Usually the number of orders accepted by credit card is limited according to the regulations of different companies. The cabin attendants are responsible for all dealings undertaken and must keep a record of all items sold. Duty-free spirits and cigarettes must not be opened on board. After arrival, passengers are required by Customs Regulations to declare all items purchased.

Passengers can also order duty-free purchases from the comfort of their own homes and take delivery of them on their next international flight. For instance, they can go to the official website of the airlines and have a look through the current duty-free catalogue and make a note of the products they intend to buy. After that they complete the order form and send it to the airlines at least 96 hours before the planned departure. The airlines will process the orders and email the confirmation to the email addresses provided.

Unit 9　First Aid
（机上急救）

Section One　Listening

Phrases in Listening

divert to 改航到…　　the inconvenience 不便之处

I. Watch the video entitled First Aid and discuss the following questions in pairs:

1. What was wrong with the passenger?
2. What did the cabin attendant do to help her?

II. Listen to the announcement and fill in the missing words.

　　Ladies and Gentlemen, I am the 1 _____ of this flight and this is an important announcement. We have a serious 2 _____ situation. There is a sick passenger on board and we need to 3 _____ to Hongqiao Airport, the 4 _____ airport, as soon as possible. Our cabin attendants will 5 _____ the cabin for landing. Our aircraft will be landing within the next 15 minutes. After landing at Hongqiao Airport, you must 6 _____ onboard the aircraft and don't get off the plane. I do apologize for the 7 _____ caused by this diversion. I'd like to thank you for your cooperation and understanding. After landing at Hongqiao Airport, we will keep you regularly 8 _____ with our plans for your onward flight today.

Section Two　Conversations

PAX: Passenger　　CA1: Cabin Attendant 1
CA2: Cabin Attendant 2

Dialogue 1　Airsickness

CA: Did you press the call button? What can I do for you?
PAX: The plane is bumping badly, and I'm very sick and feel like vomiting.

CA: Don't worry, I think you are suffering from airsickness.

PAX: What shall I do then? Is there any sick medicine on the plane?

CA: Sorry, there isn't any sickness medicine, but I can give you some more airsickness bags. If you want to vomit, you can use them. You can loosen your collar and unfasten your belt to make yourself feel comfortable. Would you like a cup of warm water and hot towels?

PAX: Sure.

CA: Here is a glass of water, and please use this hot towel to wipe your face. Let me turn up the airflow from the upper fan for you. If you vomit again, please press this call button for help. I'll be back soon. Don't worry, I will take care of you. (a moment later) Do you feel better now?

PAX: Yes, much better. Thank you.

Dialogue 2   Earache

CA: Can I help you?

PAX: Yes, I feel pain in my ears, and I can hardly hear anything.

CA: This happens sometimes when the plane is taking off or descending. Don't worry. It's because of a change in air pressure. You can relieve your earache by swallowing or eating sweets.

PAX: What else can I do?

CA: Or you just do as I show you: Pinch your nose with your fingers and close your mouth, then blow like this.

PAX: Great! It works!

Dialogue 3   A bad cold

CA: How may I help you?

PAX: I'm afraid that I've caught a cold. I have a headache, a sore throat and my nose is blocked.

CA: I'm sorry to hear that. I'll get you a cup of hot water.

PAX: Can you give me a painkiller or aspirin?

CA: Certainly. I will come back soon. Here is the medicine and a cup of water for you. Please read the instructions first to see whether it's suitable for you. You may take one tablet.

PAX: Thank you very much!

Dialogue 4   Dealing with Injuries

PAX: Help! I have fallen over. I've hurt myself!

CA: Please keep calm. Keep your arm up. Let's go to wash the cut... Is it any better now?

PAX: No, my right wrist feels terribly painful. Maybe there are some bones broken.

CA: Take it easy. The bleeding has stopped. I'll wrap it up with gauze. Please sit down and have a rest. We'll contact the airport and there'll be a doctor waiting for you when we land to examine the injury.

PAX: Thank you!

Dialogue 5　Indigestion Problem

CA1: The middle-aged man in 30D looks awful. I think he is ill.

CA2: I will go and check... Excuse me, Sir. Are you all right? How are you feeling?

PAX: Er... I don't know what's wrong... I mean I've got this awful pain.

CA2: Where is the pain? In your stomach?

PAX: Yes.

CA2: When did it start?

PAX: A few minutes ago.

CA2: Have you had this pain before?

PAX: Oh, yes. It's an indigestion problem.

CA2: How about taking some indigestion tablets?

PAX: Sure.

CA2: Take two of these, but if it doesn't improve let us know, OK?

PAX: OK.

Dialogue 6　Serious Medical Condition

CA: What can I do for you?

PAX: I've got a splitting headache. I feel cold in both hands and feet and I have pain in my stomach.

CA: Oh, I'm sorry to hear that. What can I do for you?

PAX: Could you give me something hot to drink?

CA: Just wait a moment, I'll be back soon. (later) Here is your hot water.

PAX: Thank you very much!

　　(15 minutes later)

CA: Let me help you go to the front cabin. There are some vacant seats there. I can remove the armrests and let you lie down.
　　Here we are. Sit down here. (The stewardess removes the armrest.) Please lie down. The airsickness bag is in your seat pocket. If you feel sick, you can use it, and we'll take it away later. Is it any better now?

PAX: No, I still feel rather groggy.

CA: Don't worry. I'll ask the passengers to see if there's a doctor on board. I'm sorry to tell you there's no doctor or nurse on board. But we have informed the ground staff and they'll send you to the hospital as soon as we arrive at the airport. Is that all right?

PAX: I really appreciate everything you've done for me.

CA: You're welcome. It's my pleasure.

Words in the Conversation

airsickness [ˈeəsɪknəs] n. 晕机	bump [bʌmp] n. 颠簸
vomit [ˈvɒmɪt] v. 呕吐	untie [ʌnˈtaɪ] v. 松开；解开
necktie [ˈnektaɪ] n. 领带；领结	wipe [waɪp] v. 擦；拭
earache [ˈɪəreɪk] n. 耳朵痛	descend [dɪˈsend] v. 下降
swallow [ˈswɒləʊ] v. 吞；咽	pinch [pɪntʃ] v. 捏；掐
sore [sɔː(r)] a. 疼痛的	suitable [ˈsuːtəbl] a. 合适的
tablet [ˈtæblət] n. 药片	wrist [rɪst] n. 腕关节
bleeding [ˈbliːdɪŋ] a. 出血的	indigestion [ˌɪndɪˈdʒestʃən] n. 消化不良
splitting [ˈsplɪtɪŋ] a. 爆裂似的	stomach [ˈstʌmək] n. 胃
vacant [ˈveɪkənt] a. 空缺的	groggy [ˈgrɒgi] a. 昏昏沉沉的
armrest [ˈɑːmrest] n. 靠手；扶手	

Useful Expressions

suffer from 遭受　　　　　　　　airsickness bag 清洁袋
hot towel 热毛巾　　　　　　　　stuff up 堵塞
might as well 不妨…　　　　　　lie down 躺下
sore throat 喉咙疼痛

Notes

1. airsick 晕机

    类似表达：seasick 晕船，carsick 晕车。

    机上常用表达：

    I am feeling a bit airsick.

    我觉得有点晕机。

    May I have another airsickness bag?

    请再给我一个晕机呕吐袋好吗？

    Is there any airsickness bag?

    有晕机袋吗？

    Do you get airsick?

    你晕机吗？

    Do you have any medicine for airsickness?

    你们有任何晕机药品吗？

    Could you give me some medicine for airsickness?

能给我点晕机药吗？

2. I'll page for a doctor.

   我将通过为您呼叫医生。

   Page 此处为动词，意为"通过公共广播系统呼叫（某人）"。

3. 机上常见的紧急状况：

   airsickness 晕机；backache 背痛；bleeding 出血；broken arm 手臂骨折；broken leg 腿骨折；broken ribs 肋骨骨折；burns 灼伤；chest pains 胸痛；childbirth 分娩；choking 窒息；dehydration 脱水；diabetes 糖尿病；dislocated shoulder 肩膀脱臼；earache 耳朵痛；fainting 昏厥；headache 头痛；heart attack 心力衰竭；indigestion 消化不良；nosebleed 流鼻血；shock 休克；sore throat 咽喉痛；sprained ankle 脚踝扭伤；sprained wrist 腕关节扭伤；stomach ache 胃痛；stroke 中风；toothache 牙痛；unconsciousness 失去知觉。

Section Three Language Practice

Ⅰ. **Substitution Drills**

Read the following sentences and do the same orally with given phrases.

1. Don't worry, I think you are suffering from *airsickness*.

   a. a cold

   b. an indigestion problem

   c. a fever

   d. diarrhea

2. You can relieve your *earache* by *swallowing or eating sweets*.

   a. headache—taking an aspirin

   b. heart trouble—lying down and have a rest

   c. stomachache—taking indigestion tablets

   d. nervousness—watching films

3. You might as well *sit down and have a rest*.

   a. try some airsickness tablets

   b. drink some hot water

   c. eat less food or water

   d. breathe deeply and relax

Ⅱ. Match the explanations in Column B with the words and phrases in Column A.

A	B
____ 1. injury	a. to cause an injury to ankle by a sudden movement
____ 2. nausea	b. a disease caused by the bite of an infected mosquito
____ 3. diarrhea	c. physical harm or damage to someone's body
____ 4. fracture	d. an illness in which a person's solid waste is lost and watery

_____ 5. indigestion   e. a medical condition caused by severe injury or pain that slows down the flow of blood around the body

_____ 6. sprain ankle   f. a serious medical condition in which the heart does not get enough blood, causing great pain and often leading to death

_____ 7. deep shock   g. the feeling that you are going to vomit

_____ 8. diabetes   h. a break or crack in something hard, especially a bone

_____ 9. malaria   i. pain that you get in your stomach when you have eaten food that is difficult to digest

_____ 10. heart attack   j. a disease in which the body cannot control its blood sugar level

Ⅲ. Role Play

1. A passenger is suffering from airsickness. What help do you offer him?
2. A passenger feels pain in his ears. Please help him.
3. A passenger has caught his finger on the edge of the seat and it's bleeding. How do you help him?

Ⅳ. Translate the following sentences into English

1. 飞机颠簸得厉害，我感觉难受想吐。

2. 我想您这是晕机了。

3. 对不起，我们不能提供晕机药，但是可以多给您一些清洁袋。

4. 您可以通过吞咽或者吃块糖来缓解耳痛。

5. 我头疼，嗓子疼，鼻子不通。

6. 我的右手腕非常痛。

7. 血止住了，我帮您用纱布包扎好。

8. 我感觉手脚发冷还胃痛。

9. 我可以去掉扶手让您躺下。

10. 很抱歉地告诉您，飞机上没有医生或者护士。

Section Four Announcements

Call for Doctor

Ladies and Gentlemen,

May I have your attention, please?

We have a sick passenger on board. If there is a doctor or a nurse among you, please contact any of our cabin crew by pressing the call button immediately.

Thank you!

Urgent Patient

Ladies and Gentlemen,

May I have your attention, please?

We have a passenger in need of urgent medical treatment. The captain has decided to land immediately at Changsha Huanghua Airport. We expect to land in about twenty minutes.

Thank you for your understanding!

Section Five Interview English

About Your Ambitions & Aspirations
理想与抱负

Q1: Why do you want to be a cabin attendant?
你为什么想成为一名空姐／空少？

A: I hope I can have the opportunity to meet people from different countries with different cultural backgrounds.

I have been interested in aviation service for a very long time, and I like the feeling of flying.

When I was a child I took a trip with my parents by air. I was attracted by the beautiful and elegant cabin attendants and since then I have wanted to be one of them.

Q2: Why are you interested in working with our company?
你为何对本公司的工作感兴趣？

A: Because your company has a very good reputation in the aviation industry for offering high-quality service.

Because the working conditions and environment of your company are excellent and I think it has a bright future in the aviation industry.

Q3: Why should we hire you?

我们为什么要雇用你呢？

A: I am very patient and responsible. I can make quick decisions and I am a good team-player.

Also, I can be very calm in any unexpected situations and I take regular exercise every day. I am in good health condition for any hard work.

Q4: What's your job plan for the future?

你未来的工作打算是什么？

A: Once I have enough experience I hope to get a management position and work my way up to senior management in the company.

First, I think I must adjust myself to the working environment. Then I have to learn from colleagues and gain some work experience. Finally I can become an excellent employee by surpassing others and myself.

Section Six Supplementary Vocabulary

nosebleed ['nəʊzbliːd] n. 鼻出血	sprain [spreɪn] v./n. 扭伤
diarrhea [ˌdaɪə'rɪə] n. 腹泻	nausea ['nɔːzɪə] n. 恶心
swelling ['swelɪŋ] n. 肿胀	joint [dʒɔɪnt] n. 关节
casualty ['kæʒuəltɪ] n. 病人；伤员	symptom ['sɪmptəm] n. 病状；征兆
shock [ʃɒk] n. 昏迷	cough [kɒf] v. 咳嗽
relief [rɪ'liːf] n. 宽慰；轻松	ankle ['æŋkl] n. 踝关节
eye drop 眼药水	nose drop 滴鼻水
life threatening 威胁生命的	rinse out 冲洗掉
heart attack 心脏病发作	circulatory system 循环系统
external bleeding 外出血	internal bleeding 内出血
vital organ 生命器官	pulse rate 脉搏率

Section Seven Self Study Reading

First Aid

First Aid is basic medical care given in good faith to a sick or injured passenger to maintain life and prevent further injury until professional medical care becomes available and takes over. First Aiders are not doctors or nurses. Basically, you are for the most part the first caregiver on the scene, and after assessment, you fulfil your duties under the above definition.

Principles of First Aid

In keeping with the definition of first aid, the three main principles of first aid are:
- Preserve life
- Prevent the condition from worsening
- Promote recovery

Steps of Applying First Aid

In keeping with the principles of first aid, the steps to applying it follow a well-known first aid acronym of DRABCD:
- D—DANGER
- R—RESPONSE
- A—AIRWAY
- B—BREATHING
- C—COMPRESSIONS-Perform CPR
- D—DEFIBRILLATION

DANGER: This means danger to you and the passengers who may need your first aid. This might be dangerous gas or liquid in the vicinity, a hole in the fuselage, a hysterical partner of the passenger who is panicking, or perhaps the passengers themselves have become violent. If possible, remove the danger from the passengers, or alternatively, the passengers from the danger.

RESPONSE: Before giving first aid, you must seek a response from the passenger.

AIRWAY: It means to ensure the passenger's airway is open and clear by correctly positioning them if required. You do this by lifting the chin and tilting the head back. This action lifts the tongue from the entrance to the air passage, allowing the passenger to breathe.

BREATHING: Ensure the passenger is breathing.

COMPRESSIONS: Perform CPR: If no signs of life are present after having just given the two quick breaths, commence CPR.

DEFIBRILLATION: If CPR is commenced, it means you have done so because they are not breathing. A passenger who is not breathing is considered to either have no heart beat or will soon have no heartbeat, and the heart is or is about to enter a state of fibrillation.

Remember-Never leave a passenger to whom you are providing first aid!

Unit 10 Safety and Emergencies
（安全和紧急情况）

Section One Listening

Phrases in Listening

oven fire 烤箱失火
be well trained 训练有素的
empty the whole cylinder 倒空一整筒
be confident 有自信的
in a clear and positive manner 以清晰坚定的方式
praise sb. for sth. 因为某事表扬某人
follow the fire flighting procedure 依照灭火程序
put an end to a disaster 结束了一场灾难

in the galley 在厨房
halon fire extinguisher 海伦灭火器
get panic 变得惊慌失措
give instruction 发出指令
other colleague 其他同事

Ⅰ. Watch the video entitled Safety and Emergencies and discuss the following questions in pairs:
1. Did the passenger take the turbulence seriously or not?
2. The passenger was shocked at how bad the turbulence was, wasn't he?

Ⅱ. Listen to the story of Peter's and mark the sentences True (T) or False (F).
(　) 1. There was an oven fire on Peter's flight last week.
(　) 2. Peter and his colleague were well trained in putting out fires.
(　) 3. Peter and his colleague lost control in this kind of situation.
(　) 4. Peter and his colleague didn't follow the fire fighting procedures.
(　) 5. There was a fire disaster on board the aircraft.

Section Two Conversations

PAX: Passenger　CA: Cabin Attendant　CA1: Cabin Attendant 1
CA2: Cabin Attendant 2

Dialogue 1　Turbulence

CA：Ladies and Gentlemen, we are entering an area of turbulence, so please fasten your seatbelts. Use of the lavatories has been suspended.

PAX：(standing in the aisle) But I want to take my coat out of the locker. I am a little cold.

CA：Miss, the captain has switched on the seat belt sign. Could you go back to your seat, please?

PAX：I know. I'll be OK.

CA：Miss, you must return to your seat now. We are expecting serious turbulence immediately.

PAX：It'll be fine. Why do I need to return to my seat?

CA：In order to ensure your safety, please remain strapped in. I'll get you a blanket.

PAX：All right.

Dialogue 2　Minor Fire

PAX：Come over here, Miss. There is a fire in the overhead locker.

CA：Thank you for telling me, sir. Would you please sit in that vacant seat in front?

PAX：OK.

CA1：Get the extinguisher immediately.

CA2：OK. I will get it for you right away.

CA1：I will inform the purser.

Dialogue 3　Sudden Loss of Cabin Pressure

CA：Ladies and Gentlemen, we are making a rapid controlled descent for a few minutes to a safer altitude because of a sudden loss of cabin pressure. Please return to your seats and fasten your seatbelts.

PAX：What's up? The oxygen mask dropped down.

CA：Please pull down the nearest oxygen mask towards you, hold it securely over your nose and mouth and breathe normally.

PAX：OK.

CA：You can take off your oxygen mask now.

PAX：Are you sure it's safe now?

CA：For sure. You can breathe normally once we get below 10000 feet. You are quite safe now.

PAX：That's great!

Dialogue 4　Inflating Life Jacket

PAX：Help! Could you tell me how to inflate the life jacket?

CA：Didn't you watch the life jacket demo just now?

PAX：I was asleep.

CA：You can inflate it by pulling down these tabs on the lower part of your life jacket, and if it is not inflated enough blow into these mouthpieces. Remember not to inflate it while you are in the cabin.

PAX: All right.

Dialogue 5　Emergency Landing

CA: Ladies and Gentlemen, due to the engine failure our aircraft will soon make an emergency landing at the nearest airport.

PAX: What's happening? Are we going to crash?

CA: Definitely not. We'll be on the ground safely.

PAX: But I'm really scared.

CA: There is nothing to worry about. Our captain is fully confident that we can land safely. Please obey our instructions.

Dialogue 6　Evacuation

CA: Please unfasten your seatbelts and disembark from the aircraft as quickly as possible.

PAX: Where is my handbag? I can't find it.

CA: Please leave everything behind. Come this way in a safe, orderly manner!

PAX: OK. What's this?

CA: It' an escape slide to get you quickly to the ground. Don't be scared. Jump onto it and slide down!

PAX: I can't do this!

CA: Please follow the instruction. Jump and slide down!

Words in the Conversation

ensure [ɪnˈʃʊə(r)] v. 确保
extinguisher [ɪkˈstɪŋɡwɪʃə] n. 灭火器
altitude [ˈæltɪtjuːd] n. 高度
breathe [briːð] v. 呼吸
demo [ˈdeməʊ] n. 演示
blow [bləʊ] v. 吹
competence [ˈkɒmpɪtəns] n. 能力
disembark [ˌdɪsɪmˈbɑːk] v. 下（车、船、飞机等）
scared [skeəd] a. 恐惧的

strap [stræp] v. 用带捆扎
descent [dɪˈsent] n. 下降
sudden [ˈsʌdn] a. 突然的
inflate [ɪnˈfleɪt] v. 充气
tab [tæb] n. 拉环
mouthpiece [ˈmaʊθpiːs] n. 吹气口
obey [əˈbeɪ] v. 遵守

Useful Expressions

cabin pressure 客舱压力
strap in 拴上安全带
pull down 拉下来

switch on 打开
drop down 脱落
slide down 滑下

Notes

1. Please pull down the nearest oxygen mask towards you, hold it securely over your nose and mouth and breathe normally.

   请将最近的氧气面罩拉向您，罩在口鼻处，进行正常呼吸。

2. You can inflate it by pulling down these tabs on the lower part of your life jacket or you can blow into the mouthpieces if it is not inflated enough. Remember don't inflate it when you are in the cabin.

   您可以打开救生衣下面的充气阀门为救生衣充气。充气不足时，用嘴向人工充气管里充气。记住在客舱内时不要充气。

Section Three Language Practice

Ⅰ. **Substitution Drills**

Read the following sentences and follow the same orally with the phrases given.

1. In order to ensure your safety, please *be strapped in*.
   a. fasten your seatbelt
   b. extinguish your cigarette
   c. switch off your laptop computer
   d. turn off your mobile phone

2. *We are making a rapid controlled descent for the next few minutes to a safer altitude* because of *a sudden loss of cabin pressure*.
   a. We'll return to the departure airport—the poor visibility at the destination airport
   b. We are diverting to Los Angeles Airport—bird strike
   c. We'll contact air traffic control tower—a loss of pressure
   d. We will make an emergency landing—the engine failure

3. I suppose you didn't *watch the life jacket demo just now*.
   a. notice the "No Smoking" sign is on
   b. listen to our safety announcement
   c. listen to our instructions
   d. breathe normally

Ⅱ. **Match cabin attendant's answers in Column B with passenger's concerns in Column A.**

	A	B
___ 1.	Why do I need to return to my seat?	a. For sure.
___ 2.	I'm really scared.	b. There is nothing to worry about.
___ 3.	Are you sure it's safe now?	c. Of course not. We'll soon be safe on the ground.
___ 4.	Are we going to crash?	d. To ensure your safety.
___ 5.	Why are we making an emergency landing?	e. Because there is an engine failure.

III. Role Play

1. A passenger does not know how to use the oxygen mask. Please help him.
2. A passenger does not know how to inflate the life jacket. Please help him.
3. A passenger is worried about the upcoming emergency landing. Please show concerns.

IV. Translate the following sentences into English

1. 厕所已暂停使用。

2. 请回到您的座位。

3. 为了确保您的安全，请系上安全带。

4. 请您到前舱的空座位去好吗？

5. 请将氧气面罩牢牢地放在口鼻处，保持正常呼吸。

6. 你能告诉我如何给救生衣充气吗？

7. 救生衣充气不足时可以对吹气口吹气。

8. 由于引擎故障，我们的飞机很快会在最近的机场紧急降落。

9. 没有什么可担心的。

10. 请解开安全带，快速离开飞机。

Section Four Announcements

Turbulence

Ladies and Gentlemen,

We are experiencing some turbulence. Please return to your seat and fasten your seatbelt low and tight. Please don't worry.

For your safety, lavatories shouldn't be used right now. Passengers currently using lavatories should hold firmly onto the handle. Cabin service will be suspended during this period.

Thank you!

Fire in the Cabin

Ladies and Gentlemen,

We are putting out a minor fire that has broken out in the rear lavatory of the cabin. Passengers sitting in the area of the fire please follow the cabin attendants' direction. All other passengers, please do not leave your seats.

Depressurization

Ladies and Gentlemen,

Attention: Please sit down immediately. Pull an oxygen mask firmly towards you. Place it over your nose and mouth and breathe normally. Adjust the strap to secure the mask. Put on your own mask first before assisting others. Please breathe through the masks until you are advised to remove them.

Thank you!

Section Five Interview English

About Personal Ability

个人能力

Q1: What is your greatest strength?

你最大的长处是什么?

A: I can manage my time very well and I can always get things done on time. That's my greatest strength.

I suppose my strong point is that I like developing new plans and ideas.

Q2: Do you have experience in using a computer?

你有使用电脑的经验吗?

A: Yes, I do. I have a good command of Microsoft Office.

I am experienced in operating modern office equipment.

I have mastered three computer languages: Basic, Fortran and Cobol.

Q3: Do you have any certificates of technical qualifications?

你有什么技术资格证书吗?

A: Yes. I have got a Secretary Qualification Certificate.

I have received a Tourist Guide's Qualification Certificate.

I have received an Accountant Qualification Certificate.

Q4: Can you drive a car?

你会开车吗？

A: Yes. I got my driving license when I was a sophomore.

No, I cannot drive. I am working on it now/planning to take driving lessons soon.

Q5: Do you speak English well enough to communicate with foreigners?

你能用英语与外国人交流吗？

A: I think my oral English is quite fluent. I can communicate with foreigners easily.

I worked as a volunteer in Shanghai World Expo and I was praised for excellent work, so I don't think communicating with foreigners will be a problem for me.

Q6: What quality do you think is the most important one to get success?

你认为取得成功的最重要因素是什么？

A: I think the most important one is perseverance. Only perseverance can lead a person to success.

Diligence. I am sure that a hard-working person can always succeed in the work he wants to do.

Section Six Supplementary Vocabulary

panic ['pænɪk] v./n. 恐慌；惊慌
evacuation [ɪˌvækjʊ'eɪʃn] n. 撤离；疏散
depressurization [diːˌpreʃəraɪ'zeɪʃn] n. 释压
eardrum ['ɪədrʌm] n. 耳膜
indicator ['ɪndɪkeɪtə(r)] n. 指示器
alarm [ə'lɑːm] v./n. 警报
catastrophic [ˌkætə'strɒfɪk] a. 灾难的
ditching ['dɪtʃɪŋ] n. 水上迫降
pouch [paʊtʃ] n. 小袋
impact ['ɪmpækt] v./n. 冲击；撞击
buckle ['bʌkl] n. 搭扣；扣环
mechanic [mə'kænɪk] n. 机修工
release [rɪ'liːs] v. 释放，松开
breakdown ['breɪkdaʊn] n. 故障；损坏
waste bin 垃圾箱
put out 熄灭
oxygen bottle 氧气瓶
fuel system 燃油系统
brace position 防冲撞姿态
escape slide 逃生滑梯
galley facility 厨房设备

Section Seven Self Study Reading

The September 11 Attacks

The September 11 attacks were four coordinated suicide attacks upon the United States in New York City and the Washington, D. C., area on September 11, 2001. On that Tuesday morning, 19 terrorists from the Islamist militant group al-Qaeda hijacked four passenger jets. The hijackers intentionally crashed two planes, American Airlines Flight 11 and United Airlines Flight 175, into the Twin Towers of the World Trade Center in New York City; both towers collapsed within two hours. Hijackers crashed American Airlines Flight 77 into the Pentagon in Arlington, Virginia. The fourth jet, United Airlines Flight 93, crashed into a field near Shanksville, Pennsylvania, after passengers attempted to take control before it could reach the hijacker's intended target in Washington, D. C. Nearly 3000 died in the attacks, and the 9/11 attacks have had broad and lasting consequences to military policy, politics and foreign relations. Effects have also been seen in literature, film and popular culture.

After the September 11 attacks, questions were raised regarding the effectiveness of airport security at the time, as all 19 hijackers involved in 9/11 managed to pass existing checkpoints and board the airplanes without incident. In the months and years following September 11, 2001, security at many airports worldwide was escalated to deter similar terrorist plots.

- **Changes in airport security**

Prior to September 11, 2001, airport screening was provided in the U. S. by private companies contracted by the airline or airport. In November 2001, the Transportation Security Administration (TSA) was introduced to take over all of the security functions of the Federal Aviation Administration (FAA), the airlines and the airports. Among other changes introduced by TSA, bulletproof and locked cockpit doors became standard on commercial passenger aircraft.

- **Improved security on aircraft**

Cockpit doors on many aircraft are now reinforced and bulletproof to prevent unauthorized access. Passengers are now prohibited from entering the cockpit during flight. Some aircrafts are also equipped with CCTV cameras, so the pilots can monitor cabin activity. Pilots are now allowed to carry firearms, but they must be trained and licensed. In the U. S. , more air marshals have been placed on flights to improve security.

- **Improved security screening**

Airport checkpoint screening has been significantly tightened since 2001, and security personnel are more thoroughly trained to detect weapons or explosives. In addition to standard metal detectors, many U. S. airports now employ full-body scanning machines, in which passengers are essentially X-rayed to check for potential hidden weapons or explosives on their persons.

- **Identification checks**

After 9/11, all passengers 18 years or older must now have valid, government-issued identification in order to fly. Airports may check the ID of any passenger (and staff member) at any time to ensure the details on the ID match those on the printed boarding pass. Only under exceptional circumstances may an individual fly without a valid ID. If approved for flying without an ID, the individual will be subject to extra screening of their person and their carryon items. TSA does not have the capability to conduct background checks on passengers at checkpoints. Sensitive areas in airports, including airport ramps and operational spaces, are restricted from the general public. Called a Security Identification Display Area (SIDA) in the U.S., these spaces require special qualifications to enter.

A European Union regulation has demanded airlines make sure that the individual boarding the aircraft is the same individual who checked in his or her luggage; this was implemented by verifying an individual's identification both at luggage check-in and when boarding.

Unit 11 Flight Irregularities（航班特殊情况）

Section One Listening

Phrases in Listening

flight irregularity 航班特殊情况
be encountered with 遭遇
flight diversion 航班改航
urgent medical assistance 紧急医疗救助
airport traffic congestion 机场繁忙
the air traffic tower 空管指挥部门

flight delay 航班延误
flight cancellation 航班取消
oil refueling 飞机加油
medical personnel 医务人员
take-off clearance 起飞指令
flight route 航路

Ⅰ. Watch the video entitled Flight Irregularities and discuss the following questions in pair：
1. What caused the flight delay?
2. How would your assure the passengers if you encounter a similar situation?

Ⅱ. Listen to six announcements. Match each one with a situation.

Announcement	Situation
____ Announcement 1	a. bad weather over the flight route
____ Announcement 2	b. airport traffic conjunction
____ Announcement 3	c. mechanical problems
____ Announcement 4	d. sick passengers on board
____ Announcement 5	e. refueling

Section Two Conversations

PAX：Passenger CA：Cabin Attendant

Dialogue 1 Departure Time Misunderstanding

PAX：Excuse me, Miss. Why isn't our plane taking off? The boarding pass says it will take off at 15：20, but actually it's already 10 minutes past the scheduled departure time.

CA: According to CAAC regulations, the departure time on your ticket refers to the time for closing cabin doors, not the take-off time. There are about 15 minutes between them.

PAX: Oh, I see. Thank you!

CA: You are welcome.

Dialogue 2　Delayed Departure

PAX: Excuse me. Why aren't we leaving?

CA: I'm sorry to tell you that the flight has been delayed due to mechanical maintenance. The engineers are making a careful examination of the airplane.

PAX: How long are we going to wait?

CA: It's hard to say. But don't worry about it! If we have any further information, we'll tell you immediately.

PAX: Is that so? I do hope the plane will take off soon, otherwise I will be late for my business conference in Beijing.

CA: We are very sorry for the inconvenience caused.

(a moment later)

CA: The problem has been solved. We can take off now.

Dialogue 3　Late Coming of Passengers

PAX: I've been wondering why our plane hasn't taken off yet. What's the hold-up?

CA: We're waiting for a few more passengers to come on board. We'll be leaving as soon as boarding is completed.

PAX: How irritating!

CA: I understand how you feel, but we have to wait for a few more minutes. Hopefully it won't take long.

PAX: OK.

Dialogue 4　Return to Departure Airport

PAX: Why aren't we leaving?

CA: Due to bad weather conditions, we have to return to Shanghai Hongqiao Airport and stay overnight there.

PAX: May I leave my carry-on baggage on the aircraft?

CA: You may leave all your baggage on board, but when you disembark, please be sure to take all valuables and personal necessities with you.

PAX: Who will take care of us when we arrive there?

CA: Our ground staff there will arrange free hotel accommodations for you and we will inform you of the departure time.

PAX: When are we leaving tomorrow?

CA: It depends on the weather. The weather forecast says it is going to rain all day, but we will be leaving as soon as the weather gets better.

Dialogue 5   Flight Diversion

PAX: Excuse me. How soon will we be arriving in Beijing?

CA: Sorry, Madam. Our flight has to divert to Qingdao because a passenger needs emergency medical assistance on the ground.

PAX: How long do we have to stay at Qingdao?

CA: Sorry, I don't know the exact departure time, but we have called the ground emergency services. After landing, the sick passenger will be taken to the hospital immediately.

PAX: OK, anyway. Best wishes for the sick passenger.

CA: Thank you for your understanding.

Dialogue 6   Turbulence on Route

PAX: Sir, the turbulence is very serious. Is there anything wrong?

CA: Nothing wrong. We have entered an area of turbulence and there is a thunderstorm en route.

PAX: Is it going to be like this all the way?

CA: No, I don't think so. Don't worry. The captain informed us the turbulence will probably subside in around 20 minutes.

PAX: Our flight will be delayed, right?

CA: I don't think so. Turbulence is not like a thunderstorm. Flying around a thunderstorm would delay the flight, but a turbulence won't.

PAX: Oh, I understand. Thank you.

Words in the Conversation

scheduled [ˈʃedjuːld] a. 预计的   mechanical [məˈkænɪkl] a. 机械的
engineer [ˌendʒɪˈnɪə(r)] n. 工程师   examination [ɪɡˌzæmɪˈneɪʃn] n. 检查
conference [ˈkɒnfərəns] n. 会议   solve [sɒlv] v. 解决
wonder [ˈwʌndə(r)] v. 想知道   irritating [ˈɪrɪteɪtɪŋ] a. 气人的
overnight [ˌəʊvəˈnaɪt] a. 一整夜的   valuable [ˈvæljuəbl] n. 贵重物品
necessity [nəˈsesəti] n. 必需品   accommodation [əˌkɒməˈdeɪʃn] n. 膳宿
diversion [daɪˈvɜːʃn] n. 改航   exact [ɪɡˈzækt] a. 准确的
thunderstorm [ˈθʌndəstɔːm] n. 雷雨；雷暴

Useful Expressions

scheduled departure time 计划离港时间   hold-up 停顿；耽搁
depend on 依赖；相信   weather forecast 天气预报
alternate airport 备降机场   en route 在途中

Notes

1. ... , but actually it's already 10 minutes past the scheduled departure time.

   但是实际上已经比计划离港时间晚10分钟了。

   还可以说：It's already 10 minutes behind the scheduled departure time.

2. 航班不正常的可能原因：

   bad weather in the airport /unfavorable weather over the flight route

   机场天气状况不佳/航路天气状况不好

   strike in the airport

   机场罢工

   sick passengers aboard aircraft

   机上有重病旅客

   technical problem

   机械故障

   congestion at the airport

   机场繁忙

   strong headwind over the route

   航路有强顶风

   air traffic control

   空中管制

Section Three Language Practice

I. **Substitution Drills**

Read the following sentences and do the same orally with given phrases.

1. It's already **10 minutes** past the scheduled **departure time**.

    a. 20 minutes—arrival time

    b. half an hour—departure time

    c. 40 minutes—arrival time

    d. a quarter—departure time

2. I'm sorry to tell you that the flight has been **delayed** due to **mechanical trouble**.

    a. cancelled—the engine failure

    b. delayed—the thunderstorm en route

    c. diverted to alternate airport—heavy fog at destination airport

    d. cancelled—oil leakage

3. We will be leaving as soon as **the weather improves**.

    a. we receive clearance from the control tower

    b. the mechanical problem is fixed

    c. boarding is completed

    d. the heavy fog lifts

Ⅱ. Use the conjunctions in the box to complete the sentence.

> when; if; because; after; as soon as

1. _____ we have any further information, we'll tell you immediately.
2. _____ you disembark, please be sure to take all valuables and personal necessities with you.
3. We'll be leaving _____ boarding is completed.
4. _____ landing, the sick passenger will be taken to the hospital immediately.
5. Our flight has to divert to Qingdao Airport _____ a passenger needs emergency medical assistance on the ground.

Ⅲ. Role Play
1. The flight is delayed due to a mechanical problem. The delay will be 20 minutes. Please explain the situation to the passengers.
2. The flight will be delayed because several passengers who have checked in are late for boarding. Please give the reason for the delay.
3. The flight has to divert to a different airport because there is a sick passenger on board. Please explain the situation to the other passengers.

Ⅳ. Translate the following sentences into English
1. 根据中国民航总局规定，机票上的起飞时间是指关闭舱门的时间，而不是起飞时间。

2. 很抱歉地告诉您，由于机械故障，航班延误了。

3. 工程师们正在仔细检查飞机。

4. 我真希望飞机能很快起飞。

5. 我们为造成的不便深表歉意。

6. 我明白您的感受，但我们得再等几分钟。

7. 由于恶劣的天气情况，我们将返回虹桥机场，在那里过夜。

8. 我们的地勤人员会为您安排免费宾馆住宿。

9. 天气预报说今天一整天都下雨。

10. 因为一名乘客急需地面医疗救助，我们的飞机即将改航到备降机场——青岛机场。

Section Four Announcements

Delayed Departure

Ladies and Gentlemen,

We regret to announce that our flight has been delayed due to poor weather conditions. Would you please remain in your seat and wait for further information?

Thank you!

Diversion

Ladies and Gentlemen,

May I have your attention, please?

a. Due to a strong head wind, we will have to make a fuel stop.

b. Owing to fog, (bad weather in Shanghai), Shanghai Hongqiao Airport has been closed.

c. A passenger requires urgent medical assistance.

d. Because the left engine has mechanical problems, the captain has decided to make an additional stop.

We are landing at Hangzhou Xiaoshan Airport at nine p.m. Further information will be given to you after landing. We apologize for the inconvenience.

Thank you!

Mechanical Problem

Ladies and Gentlemen,

Due to the mechanical problems we will be delayed. Our maintenance personnel are working hard to put the problems right. Please remain seated and we will keep you informed of any developments.

Thank you for your understanding!

Section Five Interview English

I. **About Remuneration**

薪酬

Q: What's your expected salary?

你期望的薪水是多少？

A： This is my first job and I don't have any experience. I think I should leave it to you to decide.

Actually, money is not the only thing I care about. You can make the decision after testing my abilities. / You can decide based on my capacity and experience.

I'd require a starting salary of at least 2500 yuan per month.

I have no definite requirement about the salary. I think you will treat me fairly on this point.

I have no exact demand for salary. Your company has been famous for good treatment to your staff and I think I'll be treated well, too. What I am looking forward now is an opportunity to work.

Ⅱ. About Vocations & Benefits

节日和福利

In this part, the interviewees can ask interviewers questions, such as:

被面试者可以这样询问面试者公司节假日和福利问题：

Q1： Could you tell me something about your welfare system?
能否介绍一下贵公司的福利制度？

Q2： Can you tell me something about holidays and time off?
能否谈谈有关节假日和休假的情况？

Q3： Do you have life insurance or health insurance for employees?
公司会给员工提供人寿保险或者健康保险吗？

Q4： May I ask what the bonuses are?
我能问一下奖金的情况吗？

Q5： Are there further opportunities for training and development?
贵公司员工有继续深造和发展的机会吗？

Section Six Supplementary Vocabulary

deicing [ˈdiːɪsɪŋ] n. 除冰
complain [kəmˈpleɪn] v. 抱怨；投诉
intensity [ɪnˈtensəti] n. 强度
erratic [ɪˈrætɪk] a. 不稳定的
compensation [ˌkɒmpenˈseɪʃn] n. 补偿；赔偿
unfavorable [ˈʌnˈfeɪvərəbl] a. 不利的；不好的
atmospheric pressure 大气压
jet stream 气流
Clear Air Turbulence 晴空湍流
mechanical problem 机械故障
on schedule 准时
departure clearance 离港许可
alternative airport 备降机场
alternative flight 备用航班
emergency service 紧急救援服务
medical assistance 医疗急救

Section Seven Self Study Reading

Flight Service Irregularities-Xiamen Airlines

1. According to the requirements of the Bureau, flight delays or cancellations information must be announced.

2. For flight delays or cancellations that result from Xiamen Airlines operations, Xiamen Airlines will:

- provide free meals
- provide books and other items for entertainment and leisure
- provide communications assistance to passengers who require it
- for delays that last more than three hours, free accommodation services will be provided to passengers. The elderly, sick and pregnant passengers, passengers traveling with young children, unaccompanied children and passengers with other special needs are guaranteed priority
- if a delayed flight arrives at the destination airport after the flight schedule ends and there is no public transportation, ground transportation should be arranged to assist passengers, according to the situation
- For flight delays of four hours or longer, financial compensation should made to passengers (including infants and children).

3. For flight delays that are caused by reasons such as weather, emergencies, air traffic control, security checks, passengers' late arrival and all other reasons beyond the control of Xiamen Airlines, Xiamen Airlines can assist passengers who would like to arrange accommodation for the period of the delay or who would like to cancel a flight from the departure airport. All costs associated with these services must be paid by the passengers themselves.

4. If a Xiamen Airlines flight experiences a diversion, delay or cancellation on route, Xiamen Airlines will provide free accommodations for passengers.

5. Proof of delay

Passengers, who require evidence of a flight irregularity, can apply for proof of flight irregularity through the on-site service counters in the terminal building, a direct sales agency or on the Xiamen Airlines website.

Unit 12 Enquiries
（乘客问询）

Section One Listening

Phrases in Listening

non-stop flight 直达航班   arrange accommodation 安排膳宿
from Shanghai to Vancouver via Seoul 从上海到温哥华经停首尔
connecting flight 转接航班   stop over 中途停留

Ⅰ. Watch the video entitled Enquiries and discuss the following questions in pairs:

1. What topic did the the cabin attendant talk about?
2. What tips did the cabin attendant give you?

Ⅱ. Listen to 5 short conversations and choose the best answer.

1. Asking for information about the flight

   Q：How long is the stop over? （   ）

   A. One day.   B. An hour.
   C. One week.   D. One night.

2. Asking for information about a connecting flight

   Q：Where can the passenger board the connection flight? （   ）

   A. In the departure lounge.   B. At the check-in counter.
   C. At the information desk.   D. He isn't given the answer.

3. Missing a connecting flight

   Q：What will happen if they miss the connecting flight? （   ）

   A. They need to return home.
   B. They have to cancel their travel plans.
   C. They will be arranged by the ticket counter.
   D. They have no idea.

4. Enquiring about the stop over

Q: What does the passenger ask for? (   )
A. He asks if he can take a direct flight to Chicago.
B. He asks if he can take a non-stop flight to Chicago.
C. He asks if he can have a direct flight to Chicago.
D. He asks if he can break his journey at Chicago.

5. Enquiring flight information

Q: What time does the non-stop flight depart? (   )
A. 10: 30a. m.   B. 3p. m.   C. 2p. m.   D. 10a. m.

Section Two Conversations

PAX: Passenger   CA: Cabin Attendant

Dialogue 1 Upgrade

PAX: I am a holder of your airline's gold card. Can you upgrade me to the Business Class on board?

CA: Sorry, I'm afraid we don't have the authority to do that. Only the ground staff can authorize upgrading at the airport terminal. I suggest you check with the information counter.

PAX: Then, can you accumulate mileage for me now?

CA: I'm sorry to tell you that we don't have this service on board, either. You may show your boarding pass and your card to the ground staff at the service counter in the terminal building.

PAX: OK.

Dialogue 2 Club Membership

PAX: Could you please tell me how to become a member of Eastern Miles Club?

CA: If you want to join Eastern Miles Club, you should fill in the application form first and take our flight as often as possible to accumulate your mileage.

Dialogue 3 Flight Time, Distance and Temperature

PAX: How far is it from Shanghai to Beijing? How long does the flight take?

CA: The flying distance is 1146 kilometers, and the flight time is about one hour and forty minutes.

PAX: Could you tell me the temperature in Beijing?

CA: The ground temperature there is minus 5 degrees centigrade to 3 degrees centigrade.

Dialogue 4 Lost Item

PAX: Excuse me, Miss. I was in such a hurry that I left my handbag at the boarding gate.

CA: Please tell me when and where you lost it and what kind of bag it is. We will ask our captain to tell the ground staff to look for it.

PAX: I put it on the chair around boarding gate 8 an hour ago and it is a small brown leather purse with the logo "Dior" on it.

CA: OK. Please write down your name, address and telephone number on this paper. If we find your bag, we will contact you right away.

PAX: I'm sorry for the trouble.

CA: No problem at all.

Dialogue 5   Flight Information

PAX: Hi, Can I ask you a few questions?

CA: Yes, go ahead.

PAX: How soon will we arrive in Paris?

CA: In about 5 hours.

PAX: What is the current altitude?

CA: It's about 9000 meters.

PAX: What kind of aircraft is this?

CA: Our plane is Airbus 320, made in France.

PAX: How many seats are there on this aircraft?

CA: There are 8 First Class seats and 150 Economy Class seats on board.

PAX: How many crew members are there on board today?

CA: There are 6 cabin attendants and 3 pilots.

Dialogue 6   Filling in the Disembarkation Card

PAX: Could you spare me a few minutes, please?

CA: Yes? What can I do for you?

PAX: This is my first international flight and I don't know how to fill in the disembarkation card.

CA: Okay, let me help you.

PAX: In this section "If you are not staying permanently what is your main reason for traveling", I don't know which box I should tick. Actually, I am here to see the doctor.

CA: In that case, you should tick the "Other" box.

PAX: OK. Thanks.

Words in the Conversation

upgrade [ˌʌpˈgreɪd] v. 升舱
mileage [ˈmaɪlɪdʒ] n. 里程
application [ˌæplɪˈkeɪʃn] n. 申请
minus [ˈmaɪnəs] n. 负号
purse [pɜːs] n. 钱包
airbus [ˈeəbʌs] n. 空中客车
tick [tɪk] v. 打钩

accumulate [əˈkjuːmjəleɪt] v. 积累
membership [ˈmembəʃɪp] n. 会员资格
temperature [ˈtemprətʃə(r)] n. 温度
leather [ˈleðə(r)] a. 皮革的
logo [ˈləʊgəʊ] n. 标志
permanently [ˈpɜːmənəntlɪ] adv. 永久地

Useful Expressions

information counter 咨询台   flying distance 飞行距离
disembarkation card 入境申请表

Notes

Eastern Miles Club 东方万里行

世界上较知名的三大联盟分别是：星空联盟，寰宇一家和天合联盟。航空联盟可提供更大的航空网络，达到代码共享，资源共用，降低成本，减少转机，积分互通的效果。常用表达如下：天合联盟 Sky Team；天合优享 Sky Priority；星空联盟 Star Alliance；前程万里 Mileage Plus；代码共享 Code-Sharing；常旅客计划 Frequent Flyer Program (FFP)。

Section Three Language Practice

Ⅰ. **Substitution Drills**

Read the following sentences and do the same orally with given phrases.

1. Our plane is ***an airbus 320, made in the European Economic Community***.

    a. a Boeing 707, a medium-sized jet aircraft.

    b. an Airbus 340-300, a wide-bodied jet aircraft

    c. a Boeing 747-300, a large-sized jet aircraft

    d. a Boeing 737-700, a medium-sized jet aircraft

2. I suggest you check with ***the information counter***.

    a. the ticket counter

    b. the booking office downtown/ in the city center

    c. the Lost and Found office

    d. the transit desk

3. The flying distance is ***1146 kilometers***, and the flight time is about ***one hour and forty minutes***.

    a. 800 kilometers—an hour

    b. 11300 kilometers—thirteen hours and fifty minutes

    c. 1670 kilometers—two hours and ten minutes

    d. 10000 kilometers—twelve hours and forty minutes

Ⅱ. **Quick responses**

Look at the model and make quick and proper responses to the following inquiries.

Model: Purser: May I see your documents, please?

            CA: Sure. Here they are.

1. PAX: Can you upgrade me to the Business Class?
   CA: _____

2. PAX: Could you please tell me how to become a member of Eastern Miles Club?
   CA: _____

3. PAX: How far is it from Shanghai to Beijing?
   CA: _____

   PAX: How long does the flight take?
   CA: _____

4. PAX: What kind of aircraft is this?
   CA: _____

5. PAX: Could you tell me the ground temperature in Beijing?
   CA: _____

Ⅲ. **Role Play**

1. A passenger wants you to upgrade him to the First Class on board. What is your response?
2. A passenger lost his bag in the terminal building. How would you help him?
3. A passenger doesn't know how to fill in the disembarkation card, please help him.

Ⅳ. **Translate the following sentences into English**

1. 你能帮我升级到飞机的商务舱吗?

   _____

2. 很抱歉,我们的飞机上没有这项服务。

   _____

3. 你能告诉我怎样成为东方万里行会员吗?

   _____

4. 飞行距离为1140公里,飞行时间大约1小时40分钟。

   _____

5. 地面温度为零下5℃。

   _____

6. 我们会让机长通知地面工作人员寻找您丢失的包。

   _____

7. 请在这张纸上写下您的姓名、地址和电话号码。

   _____

8. 如果我们找到了您的包会及时联系您。

   _____

9. 您能给我几分钟时间吗？

10. 这是我第一次坐国际航班，不知道如何填写入境卡。

Section Four Announcements

Upgrade

Ladies and Gentlemen,

　　We are pleased to inform you that there are some spare seats available in our （First Class / Business Class）. If you would like to upgrade, we will be pleased to assist you.

　　Thank you!

Lost and Found

Ladies and Gentlemen,

　　May I have your attention, please?

　　a. If any passenger has lost their suitcase （in the cabin / in the lavatory / in the terminal / at the security check）,

　　b. If any passenger has found a suitcase （in the cabin / in the lavatory / in the terminal / at the security check）,

　　Please contact the crew immediately.

　　Thank you!

Entry Documents

Ladies and Gentlemen,

　　For your convenience, we'll be showing you a video to help you complete the landing card.

　　After the video, we will distribute immigration and customs forms. Both forms need to be completed prior to arrival and submitted to Customs and Immigrations.

　　All passengers may need to declare the flight number and show the officials the tickets or boarding pass when going through immigrations.

　　Thank you!

Section Five Interview English

Occupation-related Questions I
岗位专业问题 I

Q1: In your opinion, what are the most important qualities a good cabin attendant needs?
你认为空乘人员应该具备什么样的特点？

A: To be a good cabin attendant, we need to be courteous, helpful and warm-hearted. We have to show our sincere welcome to all the passengers.

Q2: When a foreign passenger is very satisfied with your service and compliments you, what would you say in response to the compliments?
当一位外国旅客对你的服务很满意，称赞你时，你应该如何应对呢？

A: I would say, "I am so glad to hear that. It's my pleasure!"

Q3: When a foreign passenger apologizes for having done something wrong, how would you respond to this?
一位外国乘客不小心做错了事，你如何回应他的道歉？

A: I would say, I would say, "Please don't worry. It's no problem."

Q4: What are you going to do if a passenger is suffering from airsickness?
如果有乘客晕机了，你怎么帮助他？

A: I will offer the passenger a cup of water, a towel and an anti-airsickness tablet. And I would also tell the passenger where he / she can find the airsickness bag in case of vomiting. After that I would keep an eye on this passenger till he / she feels better.

Section Six Supplementary Vocabulary

enquiry [ɪnˈkwaɪərɪ] n. 查询；询问
carousel [ˌkærəˈsel] n. 旋转式行李传送带
customs [ˈkʌstəmz] n. 海关
immigration [ˌɪmɪˈgreɪʃn] n. 移民
quarantine [ˈkwɒrəntiːn] n. 检疫
limousine [ˈlɪməziːn] n. 机场大巴

information desk 问讯台   transfer formality 转机手续
transit passenger 中转旅客   ferry bus 摆渡车
re-boarding ticket 联程机票   open ticket 不定期客票
declaration form 申报单   checked baggage 托运行李
public transport 公共交通   embarkation card 出境卡

Section Seven Self Study Reading

CIQ (custom, immigration, quarantine) Forms

Another task for stewards and stewardesses during a flight is to hand out disembarkation cards and CIQ forms to foreign international passengers before the aircraft lands at its destination.

The card will ask for lots of information about the passenger such as full name, sex, date of birth, nationality, passport and visa numbers and finally the nature of the visit. Passengers may be asked to fill out various health, quarantine, customs or other declarations.

The customs declaration form, which is similar to the disembarkation card, requires additional information for instance whether the passenger is bringing into the country any items such as livestock, plants, meat and birds, or whether they have any currency over the permitted allowance. The card also asks for the total value of goods purchased in the country of departure.

Since all the forms are not always familiar to foreign passengers, airlines usually carry extra forms on each flight in case passengers make any mistakes. It is the cabin attendant's duty to assist the passengers to fill them out correctly.

Unit 13 Prelanding Check
（降落前检查）

Section One Listening

Phrases in Listening

crucial period 关键时期
final descent 最后的降落
the latche 挂锁

on alert 保持警惕
the galley area 厨房区域
come to a complete halt 完全停止

Ⅰ. Watch the video entitled Prelanding check and discuss the following questions in pairs:
1. What should cabin attendants do before landing?
2. What should they check prior to landing?

Ⅱ. Listen to the recording and fill in the missing words.

Landing as well as taking off are both crucial periods when the cabin crew has to be on 1. _____.

As the aircraft starts to make its final 2. _____, one of the last tasks that CA's have to do is to ensure the cabin and the passengers are prepared for landing. The captain will switch on the seat belt 3. _____ and the cabin attendants will usually make an announcement to say that the aircraft will be landing shortly. All passengers must return to their seats, fasten their seatbelts, return their seat back to the upright position and stow their tray table and 4. _____. The cabin attendants will check throughout the cabin to make sure everything is ready for landing.

All the food, drink and duty-free carts should be stowed away in the 5. _____ area, all the latches for each locker should be fastened, and all the overhead compartments will be checked to ensure they are securely closed. With all the above completed and with the aircraft a few minutes away from landing, there is usually enough time for one final announcement asking the passengers to remain in their seats until the aircraft has come to a complete halt.

Section Two Conversations

PAX: Passenger   CA: Cabin Attendant

Dialogue 1   Fastening Seatbelt

CA: Excuse me, Miss. Our plane is descending now. Would you please return your seat back to the upright position and fasten your seatbelt?

PAX: OK. But I feel uncomfortable with seatbelt fastened.

CA: I understand, but it's for your own safety.

PAX: OK, I will try... But it doesn't work!

CA: Let me help you. Just press the button on your armrest. I think this returns the seat to the upright position, rather than have any effect on the seatbelt.

PAX: Sure. Thanks.

CA: You are very welcome!

Dialogue 2   Opening Baggage Compartment

CA: Excuse me, Miss. Please don't take your baggage from the compartment. Our plane is about to land shortly.

PAX: The announcement said it is only 5 degrees centigrade outside. I want to have my overcoat on when leaving the plane.

CA: Don't worry. You'll have enough time to take it out after landing.

PAX: All right.

Dialogue 3   Stowing Tray Table

CA: Excuse me, Madam. Would you please return your seat to the upright position and stow your tray table? We'll be landing soon.

PAX: Sorry, I don't know how to stow it.

CA: Okay, let me show you. Just fold it up, press it against the seat back in front of you and turn the knob. Now you see, it is stowed properly.

PAX: OK! Thank you.

CA: You are welcome.

Dialogue 4   Drawing Back Window Blind

CA: Excuse me, Madam. The plane is landing soon. Would you please put up the window blind and turn off the reading light?

PAX: All right. By the way, when will we be landing at Hongqiao International Airport?

CA: In about 12 minutes.

PAX: Thanks.

Dialogue 5   Worried Passenger

PAX: Miss, will there be time for me to catch Flight MU7307 to Guangzhou today? I am a bit worried. It's due to depart at 11:30 a.m. from Shanghai Hongqiao Airport.

CA：It is 8:00 a. m. now. If everything goes as scheduled, we should land at 8:30 a. m. You should have enough time to make the connection. I'm sure you can catch it.

Dialogue 6 Aircraft Circling

PAX：Why is our plane circling around the airport? Is there anything wrong with the aircraft?

CA：No, nothing wrong. Don't worry. It's just due to the heavy fog and poor surface visibility.

PAX：When is our plane going to land?

CA：It won't take long. We'll be landing as soon as the fog lifts.

PAX：OK, I see.

Words in the Conversation

shortly [ˈʃɔːtli] adv. 立刻；马上
knob [nɒb] n. 球形把手
connection [kəˈnekʃn] n. 连接
surface [ˈsɜːfɪs] n. 地面
lift [lɪft] v.（云、雾等的）消散

overcoat [ˈəʊvəkəʊt] n. 大衣；外套
tightly [ˈtaɪtli] adv. 紧紧地
circle [ˈsɜːkl] v. 盘旋
visibility [ˌvɪzəˈbɪləti] n. 能见度

Useful Expressions

be about to 即将…
window blind 遮光板

tray table 小桌板
poor surface visibility 较差的地面能见度

Notes

1. window blind 遮光板，也可称作 sun shade。
2. It's just due to the heavy fog and poor surface visibility.
   只是因为机场有浓雾，地面能见度较低。

Section Three Language Practice

Ⅰ. **Substitution Drills**

Read the following sentences and do the same orally with given phrases.

1. Don't worry. It's just due to *the heavy fog and poor surface visibility*.

   a. the traffic conjunction at the destination airport
   b. unfavorable weather conditions
   c. the heavy thunderstorm
   d. the heavy rain

2. Don't worry. You will have enough time to *make the connection*.
   a. take your coat from the overhead locker
   b. pick up your luggage
   c. catch your onward flight
   d. manage your upgrading
3. We'll be landing as soon as *the fog lifts*.
   a. we finish the preflight check
   b. everybody has fastened his seatbelt
   c. the obstacles in the runway have been cleared
   d. we get instructions from the control tower

Ⅱ. Complete the conversation. Use the word in the word box.

> when; time; what time; how much; how; about

PAX1: Excuse me, Miss. Could you tell me the 1. _____ difference between Paris and Shanghai?

CA: Shanghai is 7 hours ahead.

PAX1: So 2. _____ is it on the ground in Shanghai now?

CA: Let me see... About half past eight.

PAX: Sorry to bother you again. 3 _____ longer before we arrive?

CA: Oh, a couple of hours.

PAX: 4. _____ exactly do we get there?

CA: About half past seven in the evening, local time.

PAX: Do you know 5. _____ long it takes from the terminal to downtown?

CA: Yes, it takes 6. _____ 50 minutes.

Ⅲ. Role Play

1. A passenger doesn't want to have his seatbelt fastened, how would you persuade him?
2. A passenger doesn't know how to stow the tray table, how would you help him?
3. The plane is circling and a passenger is getting worried. Please comfort him.

Ⅳ. Translate the following sentences into English

1. 为了您的安全，请系好安全带。
   _____

2. 我们的飞机很快就要降落。
   _____

3. 落地后您有足够的时间拿出外套。
   _____

4. 您能把座椅靠背调直，收好小桌板吗？
   _____

5. 您能打开遮阳板，关掉阅读灯吗?

   _____

6. 顺便问一下，我们什么时候能在虹桥机场降落?

   _____

7. 如果一切按计划进行，我们将在上午 8:30 落地。

   _____

8. 我肯定您能赶上转机航班。

   _____

9. 为什么我们的飞机一直在机场上空盘旋?

   _____

10. 别担心，这只是因为大雾，地面能见度低。

    _____

Section Four　Announcements

Seatbelt Re-check

Ladies and Gentlemen,

　　We are ready for landing. Please make sure your seatbelt is securely fastened and keep your cell phones on airplane mode.

　　Thank you!

Time & Descending

Ladies and Gentlemen,

　　It is 11 p.m. local time. We will be landing at Shanghai Hongqiao International Airport in about 20 minutes. The ground temperature is 15 degrees Celsius or 59 degrees Fahrenheit.

　　We will start to descend in a few minutes. Please fasten your seatbelt, open the window shade, put the tray table in place, bring your seat to the upright position and unplug your headphones and electronic devices. Please make sure the large portable electronic devices are stowed properly. The lavatories will be closing soon.

　　Thank you!

Section Five Interview English

Occupation-related Questions II

岗位专业问题 II

Q1: What you are going to do if a passenger asks you some personal questions?

如果有乘客问你一些比较私人的问题，你怎么办？

A: I will keep smiling and politely refuse to answer. I will tell the passenger that I am working now and wish him/her a pleasant journey.

Q2: If a passenger is smoking in the cabin, how would you stop him?

如果一名乘客正在客舱内吸烟，你将如何制止他？

A: I would say to this passenger, "Excuse me, Sir. Would you please put off your cigarette immediately? According to the government regulations, smoking is forbidden on all flights. It is very dangerous. Thank you for your understanding."

Q3: Why do you want to be a cabin attendant?

你为什么想成为一名空乘人员？

A: I like the idea of the exciting lifestyle of cabin attendants. I've never enjoyed a quiet lifestyle and I really enjoy working as part of a team.

Q4: What would you do if an older lady passenger seemed upset and appeared to be crying?

如果你发现一位年纪大的女乘客看起来很沮丧好像要哭了，你会怎么做？

A: I would offer her a tissue and a glass of water. I would ask her if she needed anything else. If she said no, I would keep an eye on her but not say anything more.

Section Six Supplementary Vocabulary

standstill ['stændstɪl] n. 停止；停顿
collect [kəˈlekt] v. 收集
stow [stəʊ] v. 收藏；装载
interline counter 中转柜台

unfasten [ʌnˈfɑːsn] v. 松开；解开
temporary ['temprəri] a. 临时的
subway [ˈsʌbweɪ] n. 地铁

Section Seven Self Study Reading

Cabin Preparation

As the aircraft starts to make its final descent, one of the last tasks that cabin attendants have to do is to ensure the cabin and the passengers are prepared for landing. The captain will switch on the sea tbelt sign and the cabin attendants will usually make an announcement to say that the aircraft will be landing shortly. All passengers must return to their seats, fasten their seatbelts and place their seats and tables in the upright position. The cabin attendants will check throughout the cabin to make sure that everything is ready for landing.

- All the food, drink and duty-free carts should be stowed away in the galley area.
- All the latches for each locker should be fastened.
- All the overhead compartments will be checked to ensure they are securely closed.

With all the above completed and with the aircraft just minutes away from landing, there is usually enough time for one final announcement asking passengers to remain in their seats until the aircraft has come to a complete stop.

Unit 14 After Landing
（降落之后）

Section One   Listening

Phrases in Listening

Melbourne International Airport 墨尔本国际机场   proceed to ... 继续去…
assigned position 指定位置   disembark from 从…下机

Ⅰ. **Watch the video entitled After Landing and discuss the following questions in pairs:**

1. How did the cabin attendant feel at the beginning of the flight?
2. What did the old lady say to the cabin attendant after landing?

Ⅱ. **Listen to the captain's landing announcement and choose the best answer.**

1. What's the destination country?
   1. Australia   B. Sydney   C. Canada   D. the U. S. A
2. When are the passengers allowed to remove their seatbelts?
   A. When the purser tells them to do so.
   B. Not until the fasten seatbelt sign goes off.
   C. When the plane is taxiing.
   D. Whenever they want to.
3. When are the passengers allowed to use their cellphones?
   A. When they remove their seatbelts.
   B. Not until the fasten seatbelt sign is turned off.
   C. Not until they leave the plane.
   D. Before they disembark.
4. What should the transit passengers do?
   A. They should claim their baggage in the terminal.
   B. They should arrange for the onward flight.
   C. They should proceed to the departure hall for a ticket reservation.
   D. They should leave the departure lounge.

5. Where can passengers disembark?

   A. From the forward exit.

   B. Just follow the cabin attendant.

   C. From the front door.

   D. From both the forward and rear exits.

Section Two Conversations

P1: Passenger1   P2: Passenger2

PAX: Passenger   CA: Cabin Attendant

Dialogue 1 Hurried Passenger

CA: Excuse me, Madam. Please don't stand up until the aircraft comes to a complete stop.

PAX: When can we get off the plane? My friends are waiting for me.

CA: You can't disembark until the boarding bridge is in position.

PAX: All right. I'll wait.

Dialogue 2 Transit Passenger

PAX: Excuse me, I'm a transit passenger. Do I have to take all my belongings with me when I leave the plane here?

CA: Yes. You are changing flights at this airport, so you have to take all your belongings.

PAX: My destination is Paris. Where should I go now?

CA: You may go to the transfer counter at the terminal building to check your reservation. There's a shuttle bus near the aircraft to send you to the terminal building. Have you checked your baggage to your final destination?

PAX: Yes, I have. Do I have to change to another airplane?

CA: Yes, you will have to board another airplane.

PAX: How long do I have to stay here for the connecting flight?

CA: You will stay in the terminal building for about four hours before boarding another airplane. If you have any questions, don't hesitate to ask the ground staff and they will be glad to help you.

Dialogue 3 Continuing the Flight

PAX: Miss, I'm continuing on the flight with you to Kunming. Can I disembark after arriving at Nanchang?

CA: No. I'm afraid you have to wait on board because your boarding pass can't be reused here.

PAX: I see. Then how long will we stay here?

CA: The plane will stay here for about half an hour.

PAX: Thanks a lot.

Dialogue 4 Airport Transportation

PAX: Excuse me, It's my first time in Shanghai. Could you please tell me how to go to Zhongshan Park?

CA: OK. Outside the terminal building, there is a shuttle bus that can take you there. Or you can take the Metro Line 2. There is a metro station just inside the terminal building. There is also a magnetic suspension train connecting the metro at Longyang Road downtown. It's much faster.

Dialogue 5　Baggage Claim Area

PAX: Excuse me, Could you tell me where I can pick up my checked baggage?

CA: You can pick it up in the baggage claim area in the arrival hall. The airport shuttle bus will take you there. When you get off the bus, you will see signs to the baggage claim area as well as the exit. If you follow the directions, you will find your bags. Have a nice stay in San Francisco!

PAX: Thank you!

Dialogue 6　Polite Refusal

P1: Miss, you are so young and beautiful. Thanks a lot for your help. Please accept this small gift from me.

CA: That's very kind of you. I accept your kindness, but please forgive me if I don't accept your gift. I was only doing my job.

P2: Can I take this blanket away as a souvenir?

CA: I'm sorry to tell you that it is only for in-flight use and you can't take it from the aircraft. We have only a limited number of blankets for the seats. I hope you understand.

P2: OK. I see.

CA: Goodbye! Thank you for flying with us. We hope to have the pleasure of flying with you again.

P2: I hope so, too. Bye-Bye!

Words in the Conversation

reservation [ˌrezəˈveɪʃn] n. 预订
metro [ˈmetrəʊ] n. 地铁
suspension [səˈspenʃn] n. 悬浮
limited [ˈlɪmɪtɪd] a. 有限的

reuse [ˌriːˈjuːz] v. 重新使用
magnetic [mægˈnetɪk] a. 有磁性的
souvenir [ˌsuːvəˈnɪə(r)] n. 纪念品

Useful Expressions

boarding bridge 登机桥
shuttle bus 摆渡车
San Francisco 旧金山

transfer counter 转机柜台
magnetic suspension train 磁悬浮列车

Notes

1. Please don't stand up until the aircraft comes to a complete stop.
   请在飞机完全停止后再站起来。还可以说：
   Please don't stand up until the aircraft comes to a complete standstill.
2. You can't disembark the plane until the boarding bridge is in position.
   登机桥就位后您才能下飞机。

Section Three Language Practice

I. **Substitution Drills**

Read the following sentences and do the same orally with the given phrases.

1. Please don't *stand up* until the aircraft *comes to a complete stop*.
   a. take the baggage from the overhead compartment—comes to a complete standstill
   b. open your seatbelt—comes to a halt
   c. unfasten your seatbelt—reaches the cruising altitude
   d. move about in the cabin—gets out of area of turbulence
2. Outside the terminal building, *there is a shuttle bus* that can take you to *Zhongshan Park*.
   a. there is Metro Line 2—Hongqiao Railway station
   b. there are a few bus lines—People's Square
   c. there are taxis—the Grand Theatre
   d. there is light rail—Shanghai Stadium
3. We hope to have the pleasure of *being with you* again.
   a. flying with you
   b. bringing you good service
   c. seeing you in Shanghai
   d. serving you food and beverages

II. **Quick responses**

Look at the model and make quick and proper responses to the following inquiries.
Model: Purser: May I see your documents, please?
   CA: Sure. Here they are.
1. PAX: When can we get off the plane?
   CA: _____
2. PAX: How long do I have to stay here before the connecting flight?
   CA: _____
3. PAX: It's my first time in Shanghai. Could you please tell me how to get to Zhongshan Park?
   CA: _____

Unit 14 After Landing (降落之后) 123

4. PAX: Could you tell me where to pick up my checked baggage?
   CA: _____

5. PAX: Can I take this blanket away as a souvenir?
   CA: _____

Ⅲ. Role Play

1. A passenger wants to move to the front cabin before the boarding bridge is ready. How do you stop him?
2. A passenger doesn't know where to collect his baggage, how do you help him?
3. What should you say to passengers when they offer you gifts or tips?

Ⅳ. Translate the following sentences into English

1. 飞机完全停止之前请不要站起来。
   _____

2. 登机桥就位之前您不能下飞机。
   _____

3. 下飞机的时候我要带走所有随身物品吗?
   _____

4. 您可以到候机楼转机柜台确认你的预订。
   _____

5. 飞机旁有摆渡车送您去候机楼。
   _____

6. 如果您有任何问题尽管询问地面工作人员,他们会很乐意帮助您。
   _____

7. 航站楼外有公交车可以到中山公园。
   _____

8. 您可以告诉我哪里提取我的托运行李吗?
   _____

9. 当您到达入境大厅时,可以看到行李提取处和出口的指示牌。
   _____

10. 很抱歉,毛毯只供机上使用,不能带下飞机。
    _____

Section Four Announcements

Taxiing

Ladies and Gentlemen,

　　The aircraft is still taxiing. Please keep your seatbelt fastened until the seatbelt sign is switched off.

　　Thank you for your cooperation!

After-landing Reminder

Ladies and Gentlemen,

　　We are broadcasting the carousel information. You may collect your checked baggage at carousel Number __8__. To any customer who has a connecting flight, please go to your nearest "Transfer Service Counter". You may also contact the ground staff for further assistance.

　　(As it is raining / snowing outside, please prepare your umbrella or raincoat for disembark, and mind your steps.)

　　Thank you!

Farewell

Ladies and Gentlemen,

　　Welcome to Shanghai. (Our flight will disembark at Terminal __2__.)

　　For your safety, please keep your seatbelt fastened until the seat belt sign is switched off. When opening the overhead compartment, please take care to ensure the contents do not fall out.

　　Thank you for flying with us. See you next time.

Section Five Interview English

Occupation-related Questions Ⅲ

岗位专业问题Ⅲ

Q1：Do you know why smoking is forbidden in the cabin?

　　你知道为什么客舱禁烟吗？

A: Smoking in the cabin can easily cause fire, and the small cabin contains so many passengers that smoking will pollute the cabin air and affect other passengers' health.

Q2: Why seatbelt must be fastened during the flight?

飞行中为什么要系安全带?

A: The plane flies at a very high speed. If an emergency occurs it will cause some kind of impact. When passengers fasten their seatbelts, they can move at the same speed as the airplane to avoid injury.

Q3: How should you deal with sick passengers on the flight?

飞行中乘客突发疾病怎么办?

A: If it is not a life-threatening condition, I will first give him/her some first aid, such as medicine or oxygen. Then I will make an announcement to find out if there are doctors or other trained medical personnel on the flight who can help the passenger. If it is a very serious condition, the captain will contact the ground crew and we may make an emergency landing at the nearest airport to send the passenger to hospital as soon as possible.

Q4: Can you explain to the passenger whose ear is aching when taking-off?

起飞时一位乘客感觉耳朵疼,你能向他解释一下原因吗?

A: Don't worry. Your ears feel uncomfortable, because when the plane is taking off or landing, the air pressure in the cabin changes rapidly and that causes earache. I can offer you some chewing-gum or sweets to ease the discomfort.

Section Six Supplementary Vocabulary

fuselage ['fju:zəla:ʒ] n. 机身
jet-lag [d'ʒetl'æg] n. 时差综合征
People's Square 人民广场
halt [hɔ:lt] n. 停止
alight [ə'laɪt] v. 下来
senior passenger 年长的乘客

Section Seven Self Study Reading

After Landing

Usually, the aircraft will taxi all the way to the terminal after landing and during this time all passengers must remain seated with their seatbelts fastened until the aircraft comes to a complete standstill and the seat belt sign goes off. Only then they are allowed to get up and remove their belongings from the overhead compartments. At the same time, the captain orders the cabin attendants to "disarm the doors" or "doors to manual". The Designated cabin attendant will lift the plastic hatch, move the lever to "manual" which disengages the emergency slide from the door, and report "5 Right, door disarmed. 5 Left, door disarmed" and so on throughout the cabin by using their interphones.

It is now time for the passengers to disembark. The cabin crew position themselves at all the passenger exit doors and say "thank you and goodbye" to all the passengers.

Usually VIP, passengers in First Class and Business Class and special passengers will disembark first. If the aircraft is on a turn around, then this is the time for the cabin attendants to check the cabin prior to the next flight. Every seat position is individually checked for passenger safety cards, sick bags and in-flight magazines. The seatbelts are checked and the straps are neatly positioned. Food and drink is replenished as well as duty-free goods and the cabin and lavatory areas are cleaned throughout. If the aircraft is staying at the destination for a short time, usually the cabin attendants will just check the cabin to see if any of the passengers have left any possessions behind.

Chapter 4

Flight Debriefing

（航后讲评阶段）

Unit 15　Crew Debriefing
（航后讲评）

Section One　Listening

Phrases in Listening

safety procedure 安全程序　　　　　　　　in case of 万一
the evacuation of the aircraft 紧急撤离飞机　　managerial role 管理角色
give feedback 给予反馈　　　　　　　　　boost sales 促销

Ⅰ. Watch the video entitled The Job of Flight Attendant and discuss the following questions in pairs:
1. What is debriefing?
2. Why is debriefing so important?

Ⅱ. Listen to the passage and fill in the missing words.

The Role of Purser

1. As with a cabin crew member role, a purser is responsible for making sure that all passengers have a _____ and safe flight.
2. You will also be expected to be up to date with all safety procedures and be ready to act in case of an emergency, such as an _____ of the aircraft.
3. Aside from the standard cabin crew responsibilities, pursers also have to take on a _____ role. Depending on the airline, you would report directly to the senior cabin crew staff person but would have your own cabin to manage such as First Class or Business Class.
4. Within your _____ cabin you would be responsible for ensuring that the highest level of customer service is being provided to all passengers by cabin crew while making sure that safety procedures are being followed at all times.
5. You would also be expected to give _____ to staff members on their performance and suggest ways of improvement as well as boosting sales of onboard gifts and duty-free products.

Section Two   Conversations

(The purser, John, is holding post-flight debriefing meeting with all cabin crew members)

Purser: Good evening, everyone. I am sure you are all exhausted after this long-haul flight, so this debriefing won't be long. As you know, our flight was not very smooth, but you have all worked very hard to ensure the comfort and safety of all the passengers on board the flight. In the circumstances it was good to hear passengers saying how much they had enjoyed their flight as they got off the aircraft. So, I'd like to thank you all for the job you have done so well. Amy, you were in charge of Economy Class, any comments?

Amy: Thanks, John. Yes, it was a good flight in general. However, there were two incidents during our flight and we should talk about them now. In each case, our teamwork was not perfect. The first incident concerned shutting down the meal service because of turbulence. When the fasten seatbelt sign went on, it means…

Anna: Everyone should sit down.

Purser: Right. So, what happened, Amy?

Amy: Yes, sorry, John. I heard the "passengers and crew to their seats" announcement clearly and I just assumed that my crew would immediately help to secure the cabin and the galley. But I was wrong. Charles and Peter were dealing with a difficult passenger and they didn't do so. I should have checked on my cabin crew.

Peter: This was our fault. We shouldn't have got stuck dealing with that passenger. I should have acted more promptly.

Purser: Yes, Anna should have told you to stop and secure the cabin.

Amy: Exactly. I should have communicated better with my crew.

Purser: OK. And what about the coffee pot spillage?

Amy: During the turbulence, one trolley was still in the cabin and overturned. All the coffee pots fell off.

Purser: OK. What should you do the next time when a similar situation takes place?

Amy: As soon as I hear the announcement, I will immediately communicate with my crew to ensure that they understand the instructions. I will also make sure that the cabin and galley are secured as quickly as possible.

Purser: Right. It's vital to check your crew have understood any communication via the PA system. This is a valuable lesson we learned today. Has anyone else got anything to say about today's flight?

Erica: We should all be aware of possible problems and we should all be working for each other all the time.

Anna: Our communication and leadership must be improved.

Purser: Exactly. In my report, I'm going to recommend further crew resource management training for all the cabin crew. We've got to do better as a team.

Words in the Conversation

hold [həʊld] v. 召开，举行
exhausted [ɪgˈzɔːstɪd] a. 精疲力竭的
circumstance [ˈsɜːkəmstəns] n. 环境
incident [ˈɪnsɪdənt] n. 事件
assume [əˈsjuːm] v. 认为
promptly [ˈprɒmptli] adv. 迅速地
vital [ˈvaɪtl] a. 至关重要的

post-flight [ˈpəʊstflˈaɪt] a. 飞行后的
debriefing [ˌdiːˈbriːfɪŋ] n. 飞行讲评
comment [ˈkɒment] n. 评论；意见
concern [kənˈsɜːn] v. 涉及；关系到
urgency [ˈɜːdʒənsɪ] n. 紧迫；紧急
overturn [ˌəʊvəˈtɜːn] v. 翻掉

Useful Expressions

shut down 关闭
get stuck 困住
as quickly as possible 尽快
be aware of 知道；意识到

deal with 应付；对待
coffee pot 咖啡壶
PA system 公共广播系统

Notes

1. should do sth. 应该做某事。
   此处 should 为情态动词，具有"强制、命令、威胁"的意思，例如：You should hand in your assignment before the due time.
2. should have done sth. 本来应该做某事（但实际上没做）
3. should not have done sth. 本来不应该做某事（但实际上做了）
   此处 should 表虚拟语气，表示与过去发生的动作相反，含有责备的意味。
   He should have arrived earlier. 他本应该早点到（实际上没有早到）。

Section Three　Language Practice

Ⅰ. **Substitution Drills**

Read the following sentences and do the same orally with given phrases.

1. I should have *checked on my cabin crew*.

   a. checked and secured the cabin

   b. communicated better with my crew

   c. checked the exit door

   d. stopped talking to the difficult passenger

2. We shouldn't have *got stuck dealing with that passenger*.

   a. opened the overhead locker
   b. got involved in an argument with that passenger
   c. got trapped in that argument
   d. shouted at the passenger

3. We should *all be aware of possible problems*.

   a. be working as a team
   b. sit down and fasten our seatbelts
   c. do our last check carefully
   d. inform the captain of any onboard issues

II. Discussion and matching

Work in pairs. Discuss what you think makes the cabin and flight crew into a successful team. Match the words in column A with their meanings in Column B.

1. teamwork   a. knowing precisely each other's name
2. customer care   b. working for each other
3. problem-solving   c. working together efficiently and knowing what the others are doing.
4. crew coordination   d. regulating one's emotions, thoughts and behaviors.
5. good communication   e. working out how best to do things
6. decision-making   f. being well-trained for emergencies
7. professional training g. taking action
8. self-control   h. looking after passengers

III. Role Play

You are the purser of a long-haul international flight that has just finished during which an incident took place. You and your colleagues are now holding a debriefing to discuss the incident.

IV. Translate the following sentences into English

1. 我相信你们在长途飞行之后都筋疲力尽了。

2. 每个人都努力工作，保证了机上所有乘客的舒适和安全。

3. 我要感谢你们的出色工作。

4. 我们不应该和那个乘客一直纠缠。

5. 我应该行动更迅速一些。

6. 飞机颠簸时，一辆手推车还在客舱内，翻倒了。
   _____

7. 下次发生类似情况时你应该怎么做？
   _____

8. 关于今天的飞行，其他人还有什么想说的？
   _____

9. 我们必须意识到可能出现的问题。
   _____

10. 我们的沟通和领导必须要改进。
    _____

Section Four Interview English

Ending an Interview
结束面试

Useful sentences for ending interview

Interviewers：

1. How can we contact you about our decision?
   我们如何把结果通知您呢？

2. I'll contact you by next Wednesday. Thank you for your interest in our company.
   下周三之前我会跟您联系的。谢谢您对本公司感兴趣。

3. That's all for the interview. Please wait for our notification.
   面试到此结束。请等候我们的通知。

4. It's been nice talking with you. We will inform you of our decision very soon.
   很高兴与您谈话，我们会尽快通知您结果。

5. I will contact you about the result of the interview soon.
   我们会很快通知您面试结果。

Interviewees：

1. Thank you very much for your consideration and I look forward to hearing from you soon.
   很感谢您给我的面试机会，希望很快能收到好消息。

2. Thank you very much for your time. You can contact me by the telephone number or e-mail address on my resume/CV.
   感谢您抽出宝贵的时间面试我。您可以通过简历上的电话号码或者邮箱联系我。

3. I'll be looking forward to hearing from you. I'm very interested in this position and I believe I could do a good job for you.
   我期待贵公司的回复。我对这个职位非常感兴趣，也相信自己有能力胜任这份工作。

4. A thousand thanks for giving me the opportunity. I hope to see you again soon.
   万分感谢您给我这个面试机会。希望很快能再次见到您。
5. Thank you for interviewing me. I will look forward to hearing your information.
   谢谢您对我的面试。我等您的消息。

Section Five   Supplementary Vocabulary

teamwork ['tiːmwɜːk] n. 团队合作
coordination [kəʊˌɔːdɪ'neɪʃn] n. 协作
professional [prə'feʃnl] a. 专业的；职业的
notification [ˌnəʊtɪfɪ'keɪʃn] n. 通知
get trapped 陷入困境
well-trained 受过良好训练的

assessment [ə'sesmənt] n. 评价；评估
emotion [ɪ'məʊʃn] n. 情绪；情感
resume [rɪ'zjuːm] n. 简历

decision-making 做出决策
self-control 自控

Section Six   Self Study-Reading

A day in the life of Cabin Crew members

Here is a good insight into a day in the life Cabin Crew working on an international flight from Shanghai to Tokyo.

03:30—Good Morning

Your alarm is going off and it's time to get up for your scheduled flight to Tokyo, which is due to depart at 07:00 a.m. You apply your make up, put on your uniform and make sure your appearance is perfect (Even at 04:00 in the morning!). Cabin Crew need to check in at least 1 hour and 30 minutes prior to the aircraft departing, so you will need to report for work (in the briefing room) at 05:30. You arrive at Pudong International Airport Terminal 2 and catch the shuttle bus to the briefing room.

05:15—15 minutes to go before your preflight brief

Arriving 15 minutes earlier has given you time to check your cabin manual.

05:30—The preflight brief

You and the senior crew talk through the flight details. This will normally include the order in which the services will operate for the flight, your responsibilities for the day and if there are any passengers with special needs flying (i.e. you may be given the responsibility of explaining the emergency facilities to a blind passenger on the particular aircraft you are operating on) You should also be prepared to be asked questions regarding safety and emergency procedures for that particular aircraft.

06:00—Check aircraft

It's now time for you and your team to check your emergency equipment, that you have enough meals, drinks and duty-free for the passengers, and stock all the toilets with the necessary hand towels and tissues.

06:30—Board the passengers

Now the passengers are on the way, this is your final chance to check that your uniform is immaculate and presentable, all that's left to do is smiling and greeting the passengers as they board and helping them to find their seats if needed. Remember you are the face of the airline so plenty of welcoming smiles are essential.

06:50—Preparation to take off

All the passengers are now seated and the aircraft pushes back and prepares to taxi to the runway. It is now time to perform the safety demonstration so passengers can familiarize themselves with all the aircraft's emergency facilities. This will include pointing out the available emergency exits and lighting, the use of oxygen masks, seatbelts and life jacket. You will complete your demonstration by checking through the cabin ensuring seatbelts are fastened and loose articles are secure for take off. You will now take your seat for take off.

07:10—Services during the flight

Typical services that can be offered are:
- Headsets for the in-house entertainment
- Drinks service
- Meal service
- Tea & Coffee
- Cold towels offered to passengers to freshen up, after their meal
- Clearing and collecting the meal trays from passengers
- Selling duty-free items
- Immigration cards

10:40—Preparing the cabin for landing

During this time, you will also be checking the toilets to make sure that they are clean and stocked up. Deal with any questions or queries any of the passengers may have and most importantly maintain the safety and comfort of all of the passengers.

11:00—Landing in Tokyo

You now take your seats for landing.

Once you have landed back at your base airport and the passengers have disembarked, it's time to go back to the briefing room to count the money and to make sure that the amount of duty-free goods sold throughout the flight balances with the amount of cash you have taken. Once this has been done it's time to check your file for any changes to your future flying program and then you are free to leave.

Appendix

(附 录)

Appendix 1　Glossary
（附录1　词汇表）

A

aboard [əˈbɔːd]	v. 上（车、船、飞机）
accommodation [əˌkɒməˈdeɪʃn]	n. 膳宿
accumulate [əˈkjuːmjəleɪt]	v. 积累
adjust [əˈdʒʌst]	v. 调整
airbus [ˈeəbʌs]	n. 空中客车
air flow	气流
airport traffic congestion	机场繁忙
airsickness [ˈeəsɪknəs]	n. 晕机
airsickness bag	清洁袋
alcohol [ˈælkəhɒl]	n. 酒精
Alipay	支付宝
allergic [əˈlɜːdʒɪk]	n. 过敏的
allocate [ˈæləkeɪt]	v. 分配；分派
alternate airport	备降机场
altitude [ˈæltɪtjuːd]	n. 高度
amenity [əˈmiːnəti]	n. 设施
American Express	美国运通卡
another Vodka	再来一杯伏特加
armrest [ˈɑːmrest]	n. 靠手；扶手
arrange [əˈreɪndʒ]	v. 整理
arrange accommodation	安排膳宿
as clear as a bell	一清二楚
as quickly as possible	尽快
assume [əˈsjuːm]	v. 认为
at hand	在手边；在附近
application [ˌæplɪˈkeɪʃn]	n. 申请

assigned stations	指定号位
attention [əˈtenʃn]	n. 注意
audio [ˈɔːdiəʊ]	n. 音频
audio books	有声书
automatically [ˌɔːtəˈmætɪklɪ]	adv. 自动地
available [əˈveɪləbl]	a. 可获得的
aviation authority regulations	民航局规定
aviation first aid	机上急救

B

baby carriage	婴儿车
Baby meal	婴儿餐
baggage claim area	行李认领处
baggage label	行李标签
bargain [ˈbaːgən]	v. 讨价还价
be about to	即将…
be allergic to seafood	对海鲜过敏
bean [biːn]	n. 豆
be aware of	知道；意识到
be confident	有自信的
be encountered with	遭遇
be mixed with	与…混合
be sold out	卖光；脱销
be well trained	训练有素的
blanket [ˈblæŋkɪt]	n. 毛毯
bleeding [ˈbliːdɪŋ]	a. 出血的
block [blɒk]	v. 阻塞
blow [bləʊ]	v. 吹
block the way/aisle	挡住过道
board the aircraft	登机
boarding bridge	登机桥
boarding music	登机音乐
boarding pass	登机牌
boost sales	促销
bother [ˈbɒðə(r)]	v. 打扰
breathe [briːð]	v. 呼吸
briefing [ˈbriːfɪŋ]	n. 准备会
bump [bʌmp]	n. 颠簸

Business Class	商务舱
Business Class passengers	商务舱乘客
by cash	现金支付
by credit card	信用卡支付

C

CAAC (Civil Aviation Administration of China)	中国民航总局
cabin crew	乘务组
cabin crew manuals	乘务员手册
Cabin Log Book (CLB)	客舱记录本
cabin pressure	客舱压力
CAD (Canadian dollar)	加拿大元
call button	呼叫按钮
can [kæn]	n. 罐头
cash [kæʃ]	n. 现金
catalogue [ˈkætəlɒg]	n. 目录
catering items	餐饮物品
care for	喜欢
centigrade [ˈsentɪgreɪd]	n. 摄氏度
channel [ˈtʃænl]	n. 频道
charge pal	充电宝
Charles de Gaulle International Airport	戴高乐国际机场
checklist [ˈtʃeklɪst]	n. 检查表
chew [tʃuː]	v. 咀嚼
chewing gum	口香糖
chief purser	主任乘务长
Children meal	儿童餐
China Daily Overseas	中国日报(海外版)
choice [tʃɔɪs]	n. 选择
cigarette [ˌsɪgəˈret]	n. 香烟
circle [ˈsɜːkl]	v. 盘旋
circumstance [ˈsɜːkəmstəns]	n. 环境
clarify [ˈklærəfaɪ]	v. 使清楚
classic perfume	经典款香水
clumsy [ˈklʌmzi]	a. 笨拙的
coffee pot	咖啡壶
cologne [kəˈləʊn]	n. 古龙水
come to a complete halt	完全停止

come to a complete stop	完全停止
command [kəˈmaːnd]	v. 命令；指挥
comment [ˈkɒment]	n. 评论；意见
communicate information	交流信息
competence [ˈkɒmpɪtəns]	n. 能力
compulsory meeting	必开会议
concern [kənˈsɜːn]	v. 涉及；关系到
conference [ˈkɒnfərəns]	n. 会议
connecting flight	转接航班
connection [kəˈnekʃn]	n. 连接
considerate [kənˈsɪdərət]	a. 体贴的
control handle	控制手柄
copy [ˈkɒpi]	n. 一份
cosmetic [kɒzˈmetɪk]	n. 化妆品
cosmetics package	化妆品套装
crayon [ˈkreɪən]	n. 彩色蜡笔
credit card	信用卡
crew station	乘务员号位
crucial periods	关键时期
cruising altitude	巡航高度
current blockbusters	热映大片
customs form	海关申报单

D

deal with	应付；对待
debit [ˈdebit]	n. 借方
debriefing [ˌdiːˈbriːfɪŋ]	n. 飞行讲评
dehydrate [diːˈhaɪdreɪt]	v. 脱水
demo [ˈdeməʊ]	n. 演示
demonstrate [ˈdemənstreɪt]	v. 演示；展示
demonstrator life jacket	示范用救生衣
depend on	依赖，相信
descend [dɪˈsend]	v. 下降
descent [dɪˈsent]	n. 下降
destination [ˌdestɪˈneɪʃn]	n. 目的地
destination airport	目的地机场
diet [ˈdaɪət]	n. 日常饮食
discount [ˈdɪskaʊnt]	n. 折扣

disembark [ˌdɪsɪmˈbɑːk]	v. 下（车、船、飞机等）
disembarkation card	入境申请表
diversion [daɪˈvɜːʃn]	n. 改航
divert to	改航到…
document [ˈdɒkjumənt]	n. 文件
drinks bar	饮料吧
drink cart	饮料车
duty-free catalogue	免税商品目录
duty-free item	免税商品
duty-free sales	免税销售

E

earache [ˈɪəreɪk]	n. 耳朵痛
Economy Class	经济舱
electronic device	电子设备
emergency equipment	紧急设备
emergency equipment check	紧急设备检查
emergency equipment checklist	紧急设备检查清单
emergency exit	紧急出口
emergency procedures	紧急程序
empty the whole cylinder	倒空一整筒
engineer [ˌendʒɪˈnɪə(r)]	n. 工程师
English Earl Gray tea	英国伯爵茶
en route	在途中
ensure [ɪnˈʃʊə(r)]	v. 确保
entertainment app	娱乐软件
entertainment system	娱乐系统
equipment [ɪˈkwɪpmənt]	n. 设备
EUR (euro)	欧元
exact [ɪɡˈzækt]	a. 准确的
exhausted [ɪɡˈzɔːstɪd]	a. 精疲力竭的
evacuate [ɪˈvækjueɪt]	v. 疏散；撤离
examination [ɪɡˌzæmɪˈneɪʃn]	n. 检查
extinguish [ɪkˈstɪŋɡwɪʃ]	v. 熄灭
extinguisher [ɪkˈstɪŋɡwɪʃə]	n. 灭火器

F

Fahrenheit [ˈfærənhaɪt]	a. 华氏的

far out	太棒了
fasten ['fɑːsn]	v. 系牢
favor ['feɪvə]	n. 欢心；好感
final descent	最后的降落
fit [fɪt]	v. 适合
flight cancellation	航班取消
flight crew	机务组
flight delay	航班延误
flight diversion	航班改航
flight irregularity	航班特殊情况
flight route	航路
flush button	冲水按钮
flying distance	飞行距离
flying mode	飞行模式
follow the fire flighting procedures	依照灭火程序
forbid [fə'bɪd]	v. 禁止
forgive [fə'gɪv]	v. 原谅
for the sake of	为了…
for the time being	暂时
frequent flier	常旅客
from Shanghai to Vancouver via Seoul	从上海到温哥华经停首尔
fruit before or after the meal	餐前上水果还是餐后上水果
fruit juice	果汁
fully booked	订满；客满
functional ['fʌŋkʃənl]	a. 起作用的

G

galley ['gæli]	n. 机上厨房
geographic [ˌdʒiə'græfik]	adj 地理的
get access to	获得；可使用
get panic	变得惊慌失措
get stuck	困住
give feedback	给予反馈
give instructions	发出指令
green tea	绿茶
groggy ['grɒgi]	a. 昏昏沉沉的
ground staff	地勤人员

H

halon fire extinguisher	海伦灭火器
have a special diet	有忌口
headphone ['hedfəʊn]	n. 双耳式耳机
headset ['hedset]	n. 戴在头上的耳机
help oneself	自取；自用
hesitate ['hezɪteɪt]	v. 犹豫
Hindu meal	印度餐
hold [həʊld]	v. 召开；举行
hold-up	停顿；耽搁
hot towel	热毛巾
hurt somebody	伤到某人

I

I'm raring to go	我迫不及待要走
ice cubes	冰块
in a clear and positive manner	以清晰坚定的方式
in advance	提前
in case of	万一
in case of turbulence	万一发生颠簸
in charge of	主管；负责
incident ['ɪnsɪdənt]	n. 事件
indigestion [ˌɪndɪ'dʒestʃən]	n. 消化不良
individual [ˌɪndɪ'vɪdʒuəl]	a. 个人的
individual questions	一对一问题
inflate [ɪn'fleɪt]	v. 充气
in-flight entertainment	机上娱乐
in-flight magazine	机上杂志
information counter	咨询台
interfere with	干扰
interphone ['ɪntəˌfəʊn]	n. 对讲机
in the cockpit	在驾驶舱
in the front/middle/rear cabin	在前/中/后舱
in the galley	在厨房
irritating ['ɪrɪteɪtɪŋ]	a. 气人的
It guarantees you…	保证你…

J

jasmine [ˈdʒæzmɪn]	n. 茉莉花
Johnny Walker	尊尼获加威士忌
JPY (Japanese Yen)	日元

K

keep a close eye	留心注意
kit [kɪt]	n. 装备
knob [nɒb]	球形把手
Kosher meal	犹太餐
Kung Pao chicken	宫保鸡丁

L

laptop computer	便携式电脑
lavatory [ˈlævətri]	n. 厕所
leaflet [ˈliːflət]	n. 传单
lean [liːn]	v. 倾斜
leather [ˈleðə(r)]	a. 皮革的
legroom [ˈlegruːm]	n. 伸腿的空间
lie down	躺下
lift [lɪft]	v. (云、雾等的) 消散
limited [ˈlɪmɪtɪd]	a. 有限的
liquor [ˈlɪkə(r)]	n. 烈性酒
liter [ˈliːtə(r)]	n. (容量单位) 升
lithium [ˈlɪθiəm]	n. 锂
logo [ˈləʊgəʊ]	n. 标志
long-haul flight	长途航班
lots of legroom	很多放脚的空间

M

magazine rack	杂志架
magnetic [mæɡˈnetɪk]	a. 有磁性的
magnetic suspension train	磁悬浮列车
main dish	主菜
managerial role	管理角色
marked price	标价
mash [mæʃ]	v. 捣碎

mashed potatoes	土豆泥
Master Card	万事达卡
mechanical [məˈkænɪkl]	a. 机械的
medical personnel	医务人员
medium-haul aircraft	中程航班
membership [ˈmembəʃɪp]	n. 会员资格
metro [ˈmetrəʊ]	n. 地铁
might as well	不妨…
mileage [ˈmaɪlɪdʒ]	n. 里程
mineral water	矿泉水
minus [ˈmaɪnəs]	n. 负号
mobile phone	移动电话
modern tablet	现代平板电脑
mouthpiece [ˈmaʊθpiːs]	n. 吹气口
Muslim meal	穆斯林餐

N

napkin [ˈnæpkɪn]	n. 餐巾纸
navigation [ˌnævɪˈgeɪʃn]	n. 导航
navigation and communication system	导航和通讯系统
nearby [ˌnɪəˈbaɪ]	a. 在附近的
necessary [ˈnesəsəri]	a. 必要的
necessity [nəˈsesəti]	n. 必需品
necktie [ˈnektaɪ]	n. 领带；领结
non-stop flight	直达航班
notice [ˈnəʊtɪs]	v. 注意

O

obey [əˈbeɪ]	v. 遵守
observe [əbˈzɜːv]	v. 遵守
official [əˈfɪʃl]	a. 正式的
oil refueling	飞机加油
on alert	保持警惕
ordinary food	普通餐
organize workload	安排工作
other colleagues	其他同事
our first priority	我们首要职责
oven [ˈʌvn]	n. 烤箱

oven fire	烤箱失火
overcoat [ˈəʊvəkəʊt]	n. 大衣；外套
overnight [ˌəʊvəˈnaɪt]	a. 一整夜的
overturn [ˌəʊvəˈtɜːn]	v. 翻掉
oxygen mask	氧气面罩

P

particular [pəˈtɪkjələ(r)]	a. 特别的
PA system	公共广播系统
people's currency	人民币
peppermint [ˈpepəmɪnt]	n. 薄荷
perfume [ˈpɜːfjuːm]	n. 香水
permanently [ˈpɜːmənəntlɪ]	adv. 永久地
persuade [pəˈsweɪd]	v. 说服
pick up	拿；取
pinch [pɪntʃ]	v. 捏；掐
plug [plʌg]	v. 插入
poor surface visibility	较差的地面能见度
portion [ˈpɔːʃn]	n. 一部分
post-flight [ˈpəʊstflˈaɪt]	a. 飞行后的
potential nose gear collapse	潜在前起落架故障
praise sb. for sth.	因为某事表扬某人
preflight briefing	航前准备会
pre-ordered meal	预订的餐食
press [pres]	v. 按；压
prior to	在…之前
procedure [prəˈsiːdʒə(r)]	n. 程序
promptly [ˈprɒmptlɪ]	adv. 迅速地
properly [ˈprɒpəli]	adv. 适当地
pull down	拉下来
pure water	纯净水
purse [pɜːs]	n. 钱包
purser [ˈpɜːsə(r)]	n. 乘务长
put an end to a disaster	结束了一场灾难
put the handcart	放手推车

Q

quartz watch	石英手表

R

rate of exchange	汇率
reading light	阅读灯
reasonable [ˈriːznəbl]	a. 合理的
receipt [rɪˈsiːt]	n. 收据
recommend [ˌrekəˈmend]	v. 推荐
reduce the risk	减少风险
red wine	红葡萄酒
regulation [ˌregjuˈleɪʃn]	n. 规则；规章
refrain from	制止；抑制
require [rɪˈkwaɪə(r)]	v. 要求
reservation [ˌrezəˈveɪʃn]	n. 预订
responsibility [rɪˌspɒnsəˈbɪləti]	n. 责任
reuse [ˌriːˈjuːz]	v. 重新使用
ring the call button	按呼叫按钮
RMB (Renminbi)	人民币
run out of	没有…

S

safety and emergency procedures	安全和紧急程序
Safety Instruction	安全须知
safety procedures	安全程序
San Francisco	旧金山
scared [skeəd]	a. 恐惧的
scarf [skɑːf]	n. 围巾
scheduled [ˈʃedjuːld]	a. 预计的
scheduled departure time	计划离港时间
screen [skriːn]	n. 屏幕
seafood [ˈsiːfuːd]	n. 海鲜
seafood rice	海鲜饭
seat back	座椅靠背
seatbelt [siːtbelt]	n. 安全带
seat belt sign	座椅安全带指示灯
seat number	座位号
seat pocket	座椅口袋
secure [sɪˈkjʊə(r)]	a. 安全的；牢固的
security checks	安全检查

select [sɪˈlekt]	v. 选择
serve [sɜːv]	v. 服务
serviceable [ˈsɜːvɪsəbl]	a. 有用的
set the table	摆桌子（准备吃饭）
SGD (Singapore dollar)	新加坡元
shortly [ˈʃɔːtli]	adv. 立刻；马上
shut down	关闭
shuttle bus	摆渡车
slide down	滑下
smoke detector	烟雾探测器
smooth landing	平稳降落
solve [sɒlv]	v. 解决
sore [sɔː(r)]	a. 疼痛的
sore throat	喉咙疼痛
souvenir [ˌsuːvəˈnɪə(r)]	n. 纪念品
spare [speə(r)]	a. 备用的
spare meal	备用餐食
special meal	特殊餐食
spillage [ˈspɪlɪdʒ]	n. 溢出
spill [spɪl]	v. 溢出
splitting [ˈsplɪtɪŋ]	a. 爆裂似的
spirit [ˈspɪrɪt]	n. 烈酒
Sprite [spraɪt]	n. 雪碧
standstill [ˈstændstɪl]	n. 停止
stock [stɒk]	n. 库存
stomach [ˈstʌmək]	n. 胃
stop over	中途停留
stow away their baggage	存放行李
strap [stræp]	v. 用带捆扎
strap in	拴上安全带
stretch [stretʃ]	v. 伸展；延伸
stretch out	伸展
stuff [stʌf]	n. 东西
stuff up	堵塞
sudden [ˈsʌdn]	a. 突然的
suffer from	遭受
sugar [ˈʃʊgə(r)]	n. 食糖
suitable [ˈsuːtəbl]	a. 合适的

supplementary [ˌsʌplɪˈmentri]	a. 增补的
surface [ˈsɜːfɪs]	n. 地面
suspend [səˈspend]	v. 暂停
suspension [səˈspenʃn]	n. 悬浮
suspicious items	可疑物品
swallow [ˈswɒləʊ]	v. 吞；咽
switch [swɪtʃ]	vt./n. 开关
switch on	打开

T

tab [tæb]	n. 拉环
tablet [ˈtæblət]	n. 药片
take-off clearance	起飞指令
technique [tekˈniːk]	n. 技术
temperature [ˈtemprətʃə(r)]	n. 温度
the air traffic tower	空管指挥部门
the evacuation of the aircraft	紧急撤离飞机
the galley area	厨房区域
the inconvenience	不便之处
the latches	挂锁
the overhead bin/compartment/rack	座位上方的行李箱
the user interface	用户界面
tick [tɪk]	v. 打钩
touch [tʌtʃ]	v. 触摸
towel [ˈtaʊəl]	n. 毛巾
transfer counter	转机柜台
travel document	旅行证件
tray table	小桌板
turbulence [ˈtɜːbjələns]	n. 颠簸
TV series	电视连续剧

U

untie [ʌnˈtaɪ]	v. 松开；解开
upgrade [ˌʌpˈɡreɪd]	v. 升舱
urgency [ˈɜːdʒənsi]	n. 紧迫；紧急
urgent [ˈɜːdʒənt]	a. 紧急的
urgent medical assistance	紧急医疗救助
USD (US dollar)	美元

V

vacant ['veɪkənt]	*a.* 空缺的
valuable ['væljuəbl]	*n.* 贵重物品
vegetarian [ˌvedʒə'teərɪən]	*a.* 素食的
ventilator ['ventɪleɪtə(r)]	*n.* 通风口
video ['vɪdiəʊ]	*n.* 视频
Visa Card	维萨卡
visibility [ˌvɪzə'bɪləti]	*n.* 能见度
vital ['vaɪtl]	*a.* 至关重要的
volume ['vɒljuːm]	*n.* 音量
volume button	音量按钮
vomit ['vɒmɪt]	*v.* 呕吐

W

wardrobe ['wɔːdrəʊb]	*n.* 衣橱；衣柜
warm some milk	热点牛奶
waste bin	垃圾桶
water heater	热水
weather forecast	天气预报
weather report	天气预报
website ['websaɪt]	*n.* 网站
welcome aboard	欢迎登机
wheelchair ['wiːltʃeə(r)]	*n.* 轮椅
white wine	白葡萄酒
window blind	遮光板
wipe [waɪp]	*v.* 擦；拭
wrist [rɪst]	*n.* 腕关节
write all discrepancies	写下所有偏差状况

Appendix 2 Supplementary Vocabulary
（附录2 补充词汇表）

A

aerosol ['eərəsɒl]	n. 喷雾剂
aftershave ['ɑːftəʃeɪv]	n. 须后水
aircraft type	机型
airline ['eəlaɪn]	n. 航空公司；航线
aisle seat	过道座位
alarm [ə'lɑːm]	v./n. 警报
alcoholic [ˌælkə'hɒlɪk]	a. 含有酒精的
alight [ə'laɪt]	v. 下来
alternative airport	备降机场
alternative flight	备用航班
ankle ['æŋkl]	n. 踝关节
appetizers ['æpɪtaɪzə(r)]	n. 开胃品
arrival time	到达时间
ash tray	烟灰缸
assessment [ə'sesmənt]	n. 评价；评估
assigned seat	指定座位
assigned work	指定的工作
assist [ə'sɪst]	v. 协助；帮助
atmospheric pressure	大气压
audio program	音频节目

B

bean paste bread	豆沙面包
beverage ['bevərɪdʒ]	n. 饮料
black label	黑方（威士忌）
bland [blænd]	a. 清淡的

boarding procedure		登机手续
bourbon [ˈbɜːbən]	n.	波旁威士忌
brandy [ˈbrændi]	n.	白兰地
breakdown [ˈbreɪkdaʊn]	n.	故障、损坏
buckle [ˈbʌkl]	n.	搭扣，扣环

C

cabin attendant		乘务员
cabin door		舱门
captain [ˈkæptɪn]	n.	机长
carousel [ˌkærəˈsel]	n.	旋转式行李传送带
casualty [ˈkæʒuəlti]	n.	病人；伤员
catastrophic [ˌkætəˈstrɒfɪk]	a.	灾难的
catering company		配餐公司
Celsius [ˈselsiəs]	n.	摄氏
champagne [ʃæmˈpeɪn]	n.	香槟
charter flight		包机
checked baggage		托运行李
child packs		儿童玩具包
Chivas [ˈʃɪːvəs]	n.	芝华士酒
circulatory system		循环系统
Clear Air Turbulence		晴空湍流
cockpit [ˈkɒkpɪt]	n.	驾驶员座舱
cocktail [ˈkɒkteɪl]	n.	鸡尾酒
collect [kəˈlekt]	v.	收集
comedy [ˈkɒmədi]	n.	喜剧
compensation [ˌkɒmpenˈseɪʃn]	n.	补偿；赔偿
complain [kəmˈpleɪn]	v.	抱怨；投诉
confectionery [kənˈfekʃənəri]	n.	甜食（糖果、巧克力等）
coordination [kəʊˌɔːdɪˈneɪʃn]	n.	协作
cough [kɒf]	v.	咳嗽
cuisine [kwɪˈziːn]	n.	菜肴；烹饪
current [ˈkʌrənt]	a.	现在的
customs [ˈkʌstəmz]	n.	海关
customs regulation		海关规定

D

decaffeinated coffee		低因咖啡

decision-making		做出决策
declaration form		申报单
declare [dɪˈkleə(r)]	v.	申报
deicing [ˈdiːɪsɪŋ]	n.	除冰
delicacy [ˈdelɪkəsi]	n.	美食
departure clearance		离港许可
departure time		出发时间；离港时间
depressurization [diːpreʃəraɪˈzeɪʃn]	n.	释压
dessert [dɪˈzɜːt]	n.	餐后甜点
diarrhea [ˌdaɪəˈrɪə]	n.	腹泻
dietary [ˈdaɪətəri]	n.	饮食的
ditching [ˈdɪtʃɪŋ]	n.	水上迫降
documentary [ˌdɒkjuˈmentri]	n.	纪录片
drama [ˈdrɑːmə]	n.	戏剧
drink trolley		饮料推车
duty-free allowance		免税限额
duty-free article/goods		免税物品

E

eardrum [ˈɪədrʌm]	n.	耳膜
economy class		经济舱
embarkation card		出境卡
emergency service		紧急救援服务
emotion [ɪˈməʊʃn]	n.	情绪、情感
enquiry [ɪnˈkwaɪəri]	n.	查询，询问
erratic [ɪˈrætɪk]	a.	不稳定的
experienced [ɪkˈspɪəriənst]	adj.	有经验的
external bleeding		外出血
eye drop		眼药水

F

ferry bus		摆渡车
First Class		头等舱
flight crew		机组成员
flight route		飞行线路
footrest [ˈfʊtrest]	n.	脚踏板
foreign currency		外币
fridge [frɪdʒ]	n.	电冰箱

fuel system	燃油系统
fuselage ['fjuːzəlɑːʒ]	n. 机身

G

garlic bread	蒜蓉面包
gateau ['gætəʊ]	n. 奶油蛋糕
gel [dʒel]	n. 凝胶
get trapped	陷入困境
gin [dʒɪn]	n. 杜松子酒
ginger ale	姜汁无酒精饮料
gluten ['gluːtn]	n. 麦麸
greetings [gˈriːtɪŋz]	n. 问候

H

hand baggage	手提行李
handcart ['hændkɑːt]	n. 手推车
handle ['hændl]	v. 处理，应付
halt [hɔːlt]	n. 停止
headrest ['hedrest]	n. 头靠
heart attack	心脏病发作
herbal tea	凉茶

I

immigration [ˌɪmɪˈgreɪʃn]	n. 移民
impact ['ɪmpækt]	v./n. 冲击；撞击
inaugural flight	试飞；首航
indicator ['ɪndɪkeɪtə(r)]	n. 指示器
infant ['ɪnfənt]	n. 婴儿
information desk	问讯台
intensity [ɪnˈtensəti]	n. 强度
interline counter	中转柜台
internal bleeding	内出血

J

jack [dʒæk]	n. 插座；插口
jet-lag [dˈʒetlˈæg]	n. 时差综合征
jet stream	气流
jewelry ['dʒuːəlrɪ]	n. 珠宝；首饰
joint [dʒɔɪnt]	n. 关节

L

latch [lætʃ]	v./n. 闩上/门闩
life vest	救生衣
life raft	救生筏
life threatening	威胁生命的
limousine [ˈlɪməziːn]	n. 机场大巴
loudspeaker [ˌlaʊdˈspiːkə(r)]	n. 扬声器

M

meal tray	餐盘
mechanic [məˈkænɪk]	n. 机修工
mechanical problem	机械故障
medical assistance	医疗急救
mousse [muːs]	n. 慕斯

N

nationality [ˌnæʃəˈnæləti]	n. 国籍
nausea [ˈnɔːziə]	n. 恶心
nosebleed [ˈnəʊzbliːd]	n. 鼻出血
nose drop	滴鼻水
notification [ˌnəʊtɪfɪˈkeɪʃn]	n. 通知

O

occupy [ˈɒkjupaɪ]	v. 使用,占用
on schedule	准时
on the rocks	加冰块
open ticket	不定期客票
overhead compartment	舱顶行李箱
oxygen bottle	氧气瓶

P

panic [ˈpænɪk]	v./n. 恐慌;惊慌
Passenger Service Unit	旅客服务装置
People's Square	人民广场
pulse rate	脉搏率
pouch [paʊtʃ]	n. 小袋
preliminary [prɪˈlɪmɪnəri]	a. 预备的

professional [prəˈfeʃnl]	a. 专业的；职业的
public transport	公共交通
purchase [ˈpɜːtʃəs]	v./n. 购买
put out	熄灭

Q

quarantine [ˈkwɒrəntiːn]	n. 检疫

R

rear cabin	客舱后部
re-boarding ticket	联程机票
recline [rɪˈklaɪn]	v. 斜倚；倚靠
refreshment [rɪˈfreʃmənt]	n. 茶点
release [rɪˈliːs]	v. 释放；松开
relief [rɪˈliːf]	n. 宽慰；轻松
remove [rɪˈmuːv]	v. 拿开；移除
regular coffee	黑咖啡
reservation [ˌrezəˈveɪʃn]	n. 预订
reset [riːˈset]	v. 重启；重新设置
resume [rɪˈzjuːm]	n. 简历
retail price	零售价
rinse out	冲洗掉
rum [rʌm]	n. 朗姆酒
runway [ˈrʌnweɪ]	n. 跑道

S

safety demonstration	安全演示
safety instruction card	安全须知卡
sandwich [ˈsænwɪtʃ]	n. 三明治
Satellite telephone	（机上）卫星电话
sauce [sɔːs]	n. 调味汁；酱料
seat cushion	坐垫
self-control	自控
senior passenger	年长的乘客
shock [ʃɒk]	n. 昏迷
short-haul flight	短途航班
slide [slaɪd]	v. 滑动
snack [snæk]	n. 快餐；小吃

soda water	苏打水
souvenir [ˌsuːvəˈnɪə (r)]	n. 纪念品
sparking water	气泡水
speciality [ˌspeʃiˈæləti]	n. 特产
spicy [ˈspaɪsi]	a. 辛辣的
sprain [spreɪn]	v./n. 扭伤
standstill [ˈstændstɪl]	n. 停止；停顿
step aside	让到一边
still water	纯净水
stow [stəʊ]	v. 收藏；装载
straight [streɪt]	a. 纯的；不掺水的
strawberry ice cream	草莓冰激凌
subway [ˈsʌbweɪ]	n. 地铁
swelling [ˈswelɪŋ]	n. 肿胀
symptom [ˈsɪmptəm]	n. 病状；征兆

T

taxiing [tækˈsɪɪŋ]	n. 滑行
teamwork [ˈtiːmwɜːk]	n. 团队合作
temporary [ˈtemprəri]	a. 临时的
tequila [təˈkiːlə]	n. 龙舌兰酒
terminal [ˈtɜːmɪnl]	n. 候机楼
tip [tɪp]	n. 小费
tobacco [təˈbækəʊ]	n. 烟草
tonic water	汤尼水
transfer formality	转机手续
transit passenger	中转旅客
traveler's check	旅行支票
tray table	小桌板

U

unfasten [ʌnˈfɑːsn]	v. 松开；解开
unfavorable [ʌnˈfeɪvərəbl]	a. 不利的；不好的

V

vacant [ˈveɪkənt]	n. 空缺的
vanilla ice cream	香草冰激凌
vegan [ˈviːgən]	n. 严格的素食主义者

visa [ˈviːzə]	n. 签证
vital organ	生命器官
vodka [ˈvɒdkə]	n. 伏特加

W

waste bin	垃圾箱
well-trained	受过良好训练的
Whisky [ˈwɪski]	n. 威士忌
window seat	靠窗座位
window shade	遮阳板

Appendix 3 Answer Key
（附录3 答案）

Unit 1

Section One

Ⅱ. 1. risk   2. schedule   3. manuals   4. allocate   5. emergency

Section Three

Ⅳ.

1. Shall we begin our preflight briefing?
2. Welcome to CA853 flight to Paris.
3. I'm the chief purser in charge of today's flight. I have 10-year flying experience.
4. If you are not sure of any of your responsibilities, don't hesitate to ask us, we will be glad to help you out.
5. Flight CA853 is a direct flight, departing from Pudong International Airport at 0:15 and arriving at Charles de Gaulle International Airport at 6:40, local time.
6. Cabin service in today's flight is drinks service with breakfast and lunch.
7. According to the latest weather report, Paris will see a high of 24 degrees centigrade or 76 degrees Fahrenheit and sunny.
8. We have 12 passengers checked in Business Class and 260 in Economy Class.
9. I will remind the passengers to remain in their seats and fasten their seatbelts if our aircraft is entering an area of turbulence.
10. What will you do if the lithium battery is on fire?

Unit 2

Section One

Ⅱ. 1, 3, 6, 7, 8, 9, 10

Section Three

Ⅱ. 1. order   2. stowed   3. up   4. equipment   5. variety

Ⅳ.

1. What can I do for you, Purser?
2. I'm checking the demonstrator life jackets and oxygen masks.

3. I wonder if you can help me check the galley to see if all the galley equipment is ready to use.
4. You are supposed to check if there is anybody still inside the lavatory.
5. I've just finished checking emergency equipment, oven and water heater.
6. I have arranged the magazines and newspapers in good order.
7. I've checked all the documents necessary for the flight are on the aircraft.
8. Please help me check the entertainment system to see if they are functional including supplementary reading light, call button, video and audio, and speaker.
9. It's time to switch on the boarding music and welcome passengers to board the aircraft.
10. Purser, we've cleared the cabin.

Unit 3
Section One
II. 1. B 2. D 3. A

Section Three
IV.
1. May I see your boarding pass, please?
2. Please take this aisle to the sixth row.
3. The seat number is shown on the overhead compartment.
4. There isn't enough legroom to stretch out my legs.
5. Your baggage is too big to be put in the overhead locker.
6. The Economy Class is fully booked.
7. You may pick your checked baggage up at the baggage claim area when we arrive.
8. I'm afraid you are sitting in the wrong seat.
9. Would you mind changing seats with her?
10. Your baggage in the aisle might block the way.

Unit 4
Section One
II.
1. safety instruction card
2. assigned seat
3. emergency exit
4. the sunshade
5. tray table and footrest
6. upright position
7. fasten your seatbelt
8. reading light

9. laptop computer
10. in the closet

Section Two

Ⅳ.

1. Please do not touch the exit control handle in normal situation.
2. In an emergency, please help us open the emergency exit and command passengers evacuate from the aircraft.
3. Please extinguish your cigarette immediately.
4. This is a non-smoking flight and all toilets are equipped with smoke detectors.
5. For the sake of safety, please observe our regulations.
6. Any telephone calls on board are strictly prohibited on the aircraft.
7. Use of electronic device will interfere with our navigation and communication system.
8. Can I have access to internet during the flight?
9. The lavatories have to be closed prior to taking off.
10. Could you please tell me how to adjust the air flow?

Unit 5

Section One

Ⅱ. a. 5 b. 3 c. 2 d. 1 e. 4

Section Three

Ⅱ.

NO.	Items	Cold/soft Drink	Hot Drink	Alcohol	Way of Serving
1	beer			✓	
2	Bloody Mary			✓	
3	Pepsi Cola	✓			
4	gin and tonic			✓	
5	juice (apple, orange, tomato, etc.)	✓			
6	no ice				✓
7	on the rocks/with ice				✓
8	red wine			✓	
9	sparkling water	✓			
10	soda water	✓			
11	tea (black, green, herbal, etc.)		✓		
12	whisky			✓	
13	vodka			✓	

NO.	Items	Cold/soft Drink	Hot Drink	Alcohol	Way of Serving
14	brandy			✓	
15	champagne			✓	
16	white(tea/coffee)		✓		
17	with milk and sugar				✓
18	straight				✓
19	mixed				✓
20	bourbon			✓	
21	tequila			✓	
22	black label			✓	
23	chivas			✓	
24	cocktail			✓	
25	ginger ale			✓	
26	hot chocolate		✓		

Ⅳ.

1. Would you like something to drink, sir?
2. We have black tea, green tea, jasmine tea, peppermint tea and Wulong tea.
3. I'd like a cup of black tea, please.
4. Would you care for some soft drinks, say, green tea?
5. May I offer you some blankets or pillows to cover the wet seat?
6. Let me check if there is another seat available in the cabin.
7. Would you please return your seat back to the upright position so that the gentleman behind you may be more comfortable to have his tea?
8. I'm sorry about the delay with your drink.
9. How would you like your coffee, black or white?
10. I'm afraid the coffee will spill if there is any sudden turbulence.

Unit 6

Section One

Ⅱ. 1. F 2. T 3. T 4. T 5. F

Section Three

Ⅱ. 1. c 2. e 3. a 4. b 5. d

Ⅳ.

1. Would you like to have the fruit before or after the meal?

2. The dinner will be ready in 5 minutes. Please wait a moment.

3. Can you set your table? We are serving the dinner, sir.

4. For main dishes we have beef noodles and seafood rice, which one would you prefer?

5. I'm sorry, we are out of the seafood rice, but we still have chicken noodles.

6. Do you have vegetarian meals on board?

7. For more information, please go to our official website.

8. I could check to see if we have any spare meals for you.

9. Our passengers have a choice of Hindu meal, Muslim meal, Kosher meal, Baby meal, Child meal and Vegetarian meals.

10. Would you please warm some milk for my baby?

Unit 7

Section One

Ⅱ. 1. 125 2. 256 3. 38 4. 19; 90
   5. 53 6. 70; 17 7. 67 8. 18; 8 9. 13

Section Three

Ⅳ.

1. We have CAAC in-flight magazines and some local newspapers. Which would you like?

2. In-flight magazines are in the seat pocket in front of you.

3. My headset is not working. Can I get a new one?

4. First, press the volume button here and then press the up and down button.

5. Sorry to bother you, but I need your help.

6. Please don't touch any buttons on the control until I come back.

7. Something is wrong with my entertainment system.

8. We have amenity kits for children which contains a story-book, coloring book and crayons.

9. I want to listen to music but I can't find the music channel.

10. That's very considerate of you.

Unit 8

Section one

Ⅱ. 1. A 2. A 3. B 4. A 5. A

Section Three

Ⅳ.

1. Do you sell duty-free items on board?

2. These items are of excellent quality and reasonable price.
3. Could you tell me how many bottles of alcohol I can take into Hong Kong?
4. I'd like to buy a gift for my girl friend. Could you recommend something?
5. I have ordered a watch from your company's official online website.
6. I'm looking for a light perfume for my wife's birthday.
7. Most major credit cards such as Master Card, Visa Card, American Express are all accepted.
8. Would you like a receipt or just the credit card print-out?
9. I am sorry, we can't give you any discounts.
10. This particular item is currently out of stock.

Unit 9
Section One
II. 1. captain 2. medical 3. divert 4. nearest 5. prepare 6. remain 7. inconvenience 8. updated
Section Three
II. 1. c 2. g 3. d 4. h 5. i 6. a 7. e 8. j 9. b 10. f

IV.
1. The plane is bumping badly, and I'm very sick and feel like vomiting.
2. I think you are suffering from airsickness.
3. Sorry, we don't offer any sickness medicine, but I can give you some more airsickness bags.
4. You can relieve your earache by swallowing or eating sweets.
5. I have a headache, a sore throat and my nose is stuffed up.
6. My right wrist feels terribly painful.
7. The bleeding is controlled. I'll wrap it up with gauze.
8. I feel a chill in both hands and feet and I have pain in my stomach.
9. I can remove the armrests and let you lie down.
10. I'm sorry to tell you there's no doctor or nurse on board.

Unit 10
Section One
II. 1. T 2. T 3. F 4. F 5. F
Section Three
II. 1. d 2. b 3. a 4. c 5. e

IV.
1. Use of the lavatories has been suspended.
2. Could you go back to your seat, please?
3. In order to ensure your safety, please be strapped in.

4. Would you please go to the vacant seat in the front?

5. Please hold the oxygen mask securely over your nose and mouth and breathe normally.

6. Could you tell me how to inflate the life jacket?

7. You can blow into the mouthpieces if the life jacket is not inflated enough.

8. Due to the engine failure our aircraft will soon make an emergency landing at the nearest airport.

9. There is nothing to worry about.

10. Please unfasten your seatbelts and disembark from aircraft quickly.

Unit 11

Section One

Ⅱ. 1. d 2. e 3. c 4. b 5. a

Section Three

Ⅱ. 1. If 2. When 3. as soon as 4. after 5. because

Ⅳ.

1. According to CAAC regulation, the departure time on your ticket refers to the time for closing cabin doors, not the take-off time.

2. I'm sorry to tell you that the flight has been delayed due to some mechanical troubles.

3. The engineers are making a careful examination of the airplane.

4. I do hope the plane will take off soon.

5. We are awfully sorry for the inconvenience caused.

6. I understand how you feel, but we have to wait for a few more minutes.

7. Due to bad weather conditions, we will return to Shanghai Hongqiao Airport and stay overnight there.

8. Our ground staff there will arrange free hotel accommodations for you.

9. The weather forecast says it is going to rain all day.

10. Our flight has to divert to our alternate airport Qingdao Airport because a passenger needs emergency medical assistance on the ground.

Unit 12

Section One

Ⅱ. 1. D 2. D 3. C 4. D 5. A

Section Three

Ⅳ.

1. Can you upgrade me to the Business Class on board?

2. I'm sorry to tell you that we don't have this service on board.

3. Could you please tell me how to become a member of Eastern Miles Club?

4. The flying distance is 1146 kilometers, and the flight time is about one hour and forty minutes.

5. The ground temperature there is minus 5 degrees Centigrade.
6. We will ask our captain to inform the ground staff to look for your lost bag.
7. Please write down your name, address and telephone number on this paper.
8. If we find your bag, we will contact you in time.
9. Could you spare me a few minutes, please?
10. This is my first international flight and I have no idea about how to fill in the disembarkation card.

Unit 13

Section One

II. 1. alert 2. descent 3. sign 4. footrests 5. galley

Section Three

III. 1. time 2. what time 3. How much 4. When 5. How 6. about

IV.

1. For your safety, please have your seatbelt fastened.
2. Our plane is about to land shortly.
3. You'll have enough time to take your coat out after landing.
4. Would you please put you your seat back to the upright position and stow your tray table?
5. Would you please draw back the window blind and turn off the reading light?
6. By the way, when will we be landing at Hongqiao International Airport?
7. If everything goes as scheduled, we are going to land at 8:30 a.m.
8. I'm sure you can catch the connecting flight.
9. Why is our plane circling around the airport?
10. Don't worry. It's just due to the heavy fog and poor surface visibility.

Unit 14

Section One

II. 1. A 2. B 3. C 4. B 5. C

Section Three

IV.

1. Please don't stand up until the aircraft comes to a complete stop.
2. You can't disembark the plane until the boarding bridge is in position.
3. Do I have to take all my belongings with me when I get off the plane here?
4. You may go to the transfer counter at the terminal building to check your reservation.
5. We have shuttle buses down near the aircraft to send you to the terminal building.
6. If you have any questions, don't hesitate to ask the ground staff and they will be glad to offer you help.

7. Outside the terminal building, there is a shuttle bus that can take you to Zhongshan Park.
8. Could you tell me where I can pick up my checked baggage?
9. When you get into the arrival hall, you will see signs to the baggage claim area as well as the exit.
10. I'm sorry to tell you that the blanket is only for in-flight use and you can't take it from the aircraft.

Unit15

Section One

II. 1. comfortable 2. evacuation 3. managerial 4. designated 5. feedback

Section Three

II.
1. b; 2. h; 3. g; 4. c; 5. a; 6. e; 7. f; 8. d.

IV.
1. I am sure you are all exhausted after this long-haul flight.
2. Everyone worked very hard to ensure the comfort and safety of all the passengers on board the flight.
3. I'd like to thank you for all the job you have done so well.
4. We shouldn't have got stuck dealing with that passenger.
5. I should have acted more promptly.
6. During the turbulence, one trolley was still in the cabin and overturned.
7. What should you do next time when a similar situation happens?
8. Has anyone else got anything to say about today's flight?
9. We should all be aware of possible problems.
10. Our communication and leadership must be improved.

Appendix 4 Listening Transcript
（附录4 听力文本）

Unit 1

Section one

Ⅱ. What do cabin crew discuss at the preflight briefing?

1. A successful briefing creates an action plan for the day, communicating information between crew members and checking that we are all on the same page and reducing the risk of incidents during the flight.

2. When you arrive at your base, you will check in and make sure there are no changes to your schedule and collect any safety updates or company news. It is also wise to check your cabin crew manuals for a quick reminder of safety and emergency procedures and aviation first aid.

3. The senior cabin crew member (SCCM) will check with you that have your required items: ID, passport, manuals and introduce themselves—their task is to organize the workload and make sure the cabin crew know their responsibilities.

4. At the briefing, you will meet your SCCM and your fellow cabin crew for the flight. The SCCM will either allocate your position on the aircraft for the flight (eg. Door 1 left or R4 for example) or the most senior crew member will choose a position and then the next most senior will choose until all crew members have a working position.

5. You will then go through a safety and emergency procedures (SEP) as a team and then be asked individual questions—for example, a potential nose gear collapse on landing and how you would prepare yourself, the cabin and the passengers for a preplanned emergency evacuation.

Unit 2

Section one

Ⅱ. Pre-flight Check

Before a plane is ready to be boarded, checks need to be carried out and meetings held between flight crew and cabin crew, and then between the Chief cabin crew member and cabin crew. There may also be other briefings during the flight, before each period of duty and also during emergencies. In most countries, these meetings are compulsory and are required under national aviation authority regulations.

When the cabin crew members board the aircraft, they go to their assigned stations. After stowing away their baggage, they perform an emergency equipment check at their crew station. The cabin crew is responsible for checking the emergency equipment at their station, in lavatories, in overhead bins, in cupboards and under seats. It is the cabin crew's responsibility to write all discrepancies on the emergency equipment checklist. The assigned cabin crew member then ensures that all catering items, food, dry goods and duty-free are on-board and are stowed in their appropriate places before passengers arrive. The cabin crew member responsible for the galleys counts passenger meals and crew meals, and advises the senior cabin crew member. The cabin crew is responsible for ensuring the cabin is safe for take off. Security checks will also be done under seats, in seat pockets, in overhead bins and compartments, in magazine racks and in the crew seat area. This will also be carried out in waste bins, galley lockers and in the trolleys, as well as all areas of the toilets. Any suspicious items are reported to the senior crew member.

Unit 3

Section one

II.

(Announcement) Good morning, Ladies and Gentlemen. We are delighted to welcome you aboard British Airways. Please ensure that your seatbelt is fastened, your seat back is upright and your tray-table is stowed. At British Airways, your safety is our first priority. Your cabin baggage should be in the overhead compartment or under the seat in front of you. No smoking will be permitted on the flight.

Cabin Attendant: Excuse me, whose handcart is it? It is blocking the way.

Passenger: Oh, it's mine. I don't know where to put it. The overhead compartment is full and I've tried to put it under the seat, but it doesn't fit. Would you please help me find another compartment to put it in?

Cabin Attendant: I'm afraid you can't put the handcart in the overhead compartment. In case of turbulence, it might fall down and hurt somebody. And nobody is allowed to leave anything in the aisle as the aisle might be blocked. But don't worry, you can put it under your seat.

Passenger: OK.

Unit 4

Section one

II.

1. Hello, there, this is the exit row. Have you read the safety instruction card carefully?
2. Excuse me, sir. This is the crew seat. Would you please return to your assigned seat?
3. Hello, sir, this is an emergency exit, so no bags are allowed on the floor. Would you mind putting your bag on the overhead locker for take-off?

4. Can you pull up the sunshade, please, before take-off?
5. Could you please stow your tray table and footrest?
6. Could you put your seat into the upright position, please?
7. Madam, we're preparing for take-off, so can you fasten your seatbelt, please?
8. Sir, could you please turn off the reading light?
9. Sorry, you'll have to switch off your laptop computer during take-off or landing.
10. May I help you hang up your coat in the closet?

Unit 5

Section one

II.

1. CA: What can I get you, sir?
   PAX: What kind of fruit juice do you have?
   CA: Apple, orange, pineapple, cherry and tomato.
   PAX: Pineapple, please.
2. CA: What would you like, sir?
   PAX: Could I have a cup of tea, please?
   CA: Yes, of course. Do you mind waiting a moment? We're serving cold drinks just now.
   PAX: Oh, sorry. I'll have Sprite then.
   CA: Are you sure?
   PAX: Yes, that'll be fine.
3. PAX: Would you like a drink from the bar, sir?
   CA: Do you have wine?
   PAX: Sure. White wine or red wine?
   CA: I'll try white wine, please.
   PAX: Here you are. Please enjoy it.
4. PAX: Can I have a large glass of Coke, please?
   CA: With ice?
   PAX: Yes.
   CA: Here it is. Enjoy.
5. PAX: Excuse me, I'd like another Vodka.
   CA: Sorry, sir. We'll be landing in 30 minutes and the drinks bar has been closed. Can I get you a soft drink?
   PAX: OK. Mineral water, please.
   CA: Sure, here you are.

Unit 6

Section one

II.

CA: Excuse me, sir? Are you Mr. Brown?

PAX: Yes?

CA: Did you order a Muslim meal? Here it is. I hope you enjoy the meal.

PAX: Thank you. Can I have a cup of cold water, please?

CA: Sorry, I am afraid we've run out of ice cubes. Shall I bring you some pure water?

PAX: Sure, thanks. And I also ordered a special meal, a children meal for my son on the website of your airline, but it hasn't been served yet.

CA: Let me check. One moment, please... Here it is. It was mixed with other ordinary food at the bottom of the trolley. I'm really sorry, sir.

PAX: That's all right.

Unit7

Section one

Ⅱ. Entertainment on board

Our in-flight entertainment stands for First-Class entertainment on board. It guarantees you great entertainment on board-whether on the long-haul flights or through the Entertainment app on your mobile device or on selected medium-haul aircraft. Current blockbusters, classics of film history, music and games ensure you enjoy an interesting and entertaining flight. Passengers on long-haul flights can always look forward to a large number of TV series, audio books and CDs.

We offer you:

1. <u>125</u> films movies in up to eight languages
2. <u>256</u> TV programs
3. Large selection for families and children with many movies and TV programs, <u>38</u> Audio books and Music CDs
4. <u>19</u> "Box Sets" to enjoy featuring whole seasons of <u>90</u> TV series
5. <u>53</u> Lufthansa playlists to relax and to tune in for many destinations
6. A big selection of <u>70</u> Music CDs with an excellent selection of Rock, Pop, Classical and among them <u>17</u> is soft music
7. <u>67</u> Audio Books in German and English
8. <u>18</u> International programs, including <u>8</u> contents from the Middle East, India, Japan and China
9. Simple operation: the user interface can be operated in the same way as modern tablet interfaces and is available in <u>13</u> languages

Unit 8

Section one

Ⅱ.

1. PAX: How much is the perfume?

   CA: That's fifty-nine Euros, madam.

   PAX: No, I mean in dollars. How much is it in dollars?

CA: That's seventy-nine dollars.

PAX: Can you give me change in dollars?

CA: I'm afraid we can only give you change in Euros, madam.

PAX: All right.

2. PAX: Can I see the quartz watch?

CA: Sure, here you are. It's 100 Euros.

PAX: How much is it in Chinese Yuan.

CA: 800 RMB.

3. PAX: Can I pay for the set of cosmetics with my visa card?

CA: Sure.

PAX: Can you change into Singapore dollars?

CA: No problem. It'll be three hundred and twenty Singapore dollars.

4. PAX: I really like this necklace, but can I pay in Japanese yen?

CA: Yes, madam.

PAX: What's eighty dollars in yen?

CA: It's eight thousand eight hundred and seventy-five yen.

5. PAX: Would you mind showing me the model plane?

CA: Sure, no problem. That's eighty-nine in Euros.

PAX: How much in Canadian dollars?

CA: One hundred and fortytwo Canadian dollars.

Unit 9

Section one

Ⅱ.

Ladies and Gentlemen, I am the captain of this flight and this is an important announcement. We have a serious medical situation. There is a sick passenger on board and we need to divert to Hongqiao Airport, the nearest airport, as soon as possible. Our cabin attendants will prepare the cabin for landing. Our aircraft will be landing within the next 15 minutes. After landing at Hongqiao Airport, you must remain onboard the aircraft and don't get off the plane. I do apologize for the inconvenience caused by this diversion. I'd like to thank you for your cooperation and understanding. After landing at Hongqiao Airport, we will keep you regularly updated with our plans for your on ward flight today.

Unit 10

Section one

Ⅱ. Peter's Story

Last week we had a tough situation on the flight when an oven fire broke out in the galley. It happened very fast. There are two us when we suddenly noticed smoke coming from one of the ovens. Well, we are well trained for this kind of situation. We took immediate actions to put out the fires. My colleague switched everything off and I grabbed the halon fire extinguisher. I opened the oven door very slightly and carefully emptied the whole cylinder into the oven. The minor fire went out, just how we did during the training.

However, passengers seated near the galley got panic and were shouting "Fire". That made other passengers panic too and it was difficult to keep control. At times of this you have to be very calm and confident. I give instructions in a clear and positive manner: "Don't panic! The fire has been put out! Keep remained in your seat!" Fortunately, the purser and other colleagues offered help. They calmed the passengers and explained that the fire was out.

After that, we offered free drinks, more newspapers and any other items which passengers asked for. Some passengers were still worried because they could smell the smoke but everything went on smoothly again.

Finally, the purser praised us as we followed the fire-fighting procedures so well. We put an end to a disaster!

Unit 11

Section one

II.

1. Ladies and Gentlemen,

    We have a passenger for urgent medical assistance. If you are medical personnel, please kindly contact our flight attendant. Thank you!

2. Ladies and Gentlemen,

    The aircraft is now being refueled. Please do not use mobile phones and other portable electronic devices. For your safety, please leave your seatbelt unfastened. Thank you!

3. Ladies and Gentlemen,

    We regret to inform you that our flight is cancelled due to mechanical problems. Please take all your hand luggage with you including boarding pass, valuables and travel documents. Check that you have nothing left on board. If you need any assistance, please contact our ground staff after disembarkation. We apologize for the inconvenience and thank you for your understanding.

4. Ladies and Gentlemen,

    Welcome aboard our flight. Due to airport traffic congestion, we are still waiting for take-off clearance. Our cabin crews are ready for take-off and our captain is communicating with the Air Traffic Tower. We will update you as soon as more information becomes available. If you need assistance, please let us know. Thank you for your understanding and cooperation!

5. Ladies and Gentlemen,

The captain has just advised us that because of bad weather over the flight route, our aircraft can not take off at this time and we will have to return to the terminal. We sincerely apologize for the delay and inconvenience.

Unit 12

Section one

Ⅱ.

Conversation 1

PAX: Excuse me, is this a non-stop flight?

CA: No, I'm afraid you need to stay overnight in Frankfurt, but we will arrange accommodation for you.

Conversation 2

PAX: Excuse me, I'm going from Shanghai to Vancouver via Seoul, where can I board my connecting flight?

CA: I'm not sure. You may ask the information desk officer.

Conversation 3

PAX: I'm afraid we will miss the connecting flight.

CA: Don't worry, if we miss the flight, we can go to the ticket counter and I think they will arrange a new flight for us.

Conversation 4

PAX: Is that possible to stop over at Chicago?

CA: Let me have a look. Yes, you may break your journey here.

Conversation 5

PAX: Could you tell me some information about the flight to Sydney, please?

CA: Sure, there is a non-stop flight at 10:30 a.m. and you can also take the 3 p.m. flight, but you need to stop over in Beijing for 2 hours. Which one would you prefer?

Unit 13

Section one

Ⅱ.

Landing as well as taking off are both crucial periods when the cabin crew has to be on <u>alert</u>.

As the aircraft starts to make its final <u>descent</u>, one of the last tasks that CA's have to do is to ensure the cabin and the passengers are prepared for landing. The captain will switch on the seatbelt <u>sign</u> and the cabin attendants will usually make an announcement to say that the aircraft will be landing shortly. All passengers must return to their seats, fasten their seatbelts, return their seat back to the upright position and stow their tray table and <u>footrests</u>. The cabin attendants will check throughout the cabin to make sure everything is ready for landing.

All the food, drink and duty-free carts should be stowed away in the galley area, all the latches for each locker should be fastened, and all the overhead compartments will be checked to ensure they are securely closed. With all the above completed and with the aircraft a few minutes away from landing, there is usually enough time for one final announcement asking the passengers to remain in their seats until the aircraft has come to a complete halt.

Unit 14

Section one

II. Ladies and Gentlemen,

We have landed at Melbourne International Airport.

The plane is now still taxiing, please don't open your seatbelt until the fasten seatbelt sign goes off. Please do not turn on your mobile phone before you get off the plane. Take care when opening the overhead compartment. Your checked baggage maybe claimed in the terminal. Transit passengers please proceed to the departure hall in the terminal building to arrange your connecting flight. Now our plane has arrived at the assigned position. Please check to take all your belongings with you and disembark from the front door. Thank you for choosing our United Airlines. Have a nice day! Thank you!

Unit 15

Section one

II. The Role of Purser

1. As with a cabin crew member role, a purser is responsible for making sure that all passengers have a comfortable and safe flight.
2. You will also be expected to be up to date with all safety procedures and be ready to act in case of an emergency, such as an evacuation of the aircraft.
3. Aside from the standard cabin crew responsibilities, pursers also have to take on a managerial role. Depending on the airline, you would report directly to the senior cabin crew staff person but would have your own cabin to manage such as First Class or Business Class.
4. Within your designated cabin you would be responsible for ensuring that the highest level of customer service is being provided to all passengers by cabin crew while making sure that safety procedures are being followed at all times.
5. You would also be expected to give feedback to staff members on their performance and suggest ways of improvement as well as boosting sales of onboard gifts and duty-free products.

References(参考文献)

[1] Gerighty T. English for Cabin Crew. Heinle Cengage Learning:Summertown Publishing,2011.
[2] Liveabc互动英语教学集团. 观光旅游一本通. 北京:外语教学与研究出版社,2006.
[3] Lewis Lansford. English for Cabin Crew. Sue Eltis:Oxford University Press,1988.
[4] 范晔. 空中乘务情景英语. 北京:清华大学出版社,2018.
[5] 何志强. 民航乘务英语会话. 北京:旅游教育出版社,2007.
[6] 黄华. 民航客舱服务实用英语. 天津:天津大学出版社,2010.
[7] 教材编写组. 民航乘务英语. 北京:高等教育出版社,2006.
[8] 李玉梅,杨建. 新世纪民航乘务英语(中级)口语教程. 天津:南开大学出版社,2005.
[9] 林杨,余明洋. 民航乘务英语视听. 北京:旅游教育出版社,2014.
[10] 俞涛. 民航服务英语. 北京:中国民航出版社,2011.
[11] 张艳玲. 民航专业英语. 北京:中国民航出版社,2007.
[12] 陈根生,汤平平. 新编航空乘务人员面试英语. 北京:中国经济出版社,2015.